JOHN
GIELGUD

JOHN
GIELGUD
A Celebration

GYLES
BRANDRETH

PAVILION
MICHAEL JOSEPH

Designed by Craig Dodd

First published in paperback in 1985 by
Pavilion Books Limited
196 Shaftesbury Avenue, London WC2H 8JL
in association with Michael Joseph Limited
44 Bedford Square, London WC1B 3DP

Brandreth, Gyles
   John Gielgud
   1. Gielgud, John   2. Actors—Great Britain
   —Biography
   I. Title
   792'.028'0924   PN 2598.G45

   ISBN 09 07516 98 X

Printed in Great Britain by BAS Printers Limited
and bound by Butler and Tanner Limited.

CONTENTS

To John Gielgud

This book is a celebration of one of the most extraordinary careers in the history of entertainment. John Gielgud made his first appearance at the Old Vic in London in 1921, his first radio broadcast in 1923, his first film in 1924. By 1926 he was starring in London's West End. In 1928 he made his debut on Broadway. For more than half a century he has been a household name, revered as one of the greatest actors of our time, and in 1985, at the age of eighty-one, he is indisputably still at the top.

Gielgud was making silent pictures in the twenties. Sixty years later he is one of the world's most sought-after movie stars: since winning his first Oscar in *Arthur* at the age of seventy-eight he has appeared in at least a dozen major films and television series. Inevitably there are millions who have seen him only in the cinema or on television, but it is as a stage actor that Gielgud will be best and rightly remembered and, above all, as an interpreter of Shakespeare. For many his Hamlet, his Richard II, his Macbeth, his Lear, his Cassius, his Benedick, his Prospero, were not just remarkable performances: they were definitive. 'Never has English sounded more beautiful from the human mouth' was one verdict on his Hamlet at Elsinore in 1939 and the incomparable 'Gielgud voice' – 'all cello and woodwind', 'so distinctive yet so subtle', 'the perfect instrument for the expression of the nobility and sensitivity of the man' – has long been regarded as one of the chief glories of twentieth century theatre.

Gielgud's stage successes over a lifetime – in Shakespeare, in Chekhov, in Gordon Daviot's *Richard of Bordeaux*, in *The Importance of Being Earnest*, in *The School for Scandal*, in *Love for Love*, in Christopher Fry's *The Lady's Not for Burning*, and most recently, of course, in perfect concert with Sir Ralph Richardson in David Storey's *Home* and Harold Pinter's *No Man's Land* – have far outnumbered his failures, but Sir John would be the last to pretend that his long and distinguished career has been without its disastrous moments. I remember the first time I saw him in a modern play – Thornton Wilder's *The Ides of March* at the Haymarket in 1963 – the audience booed. Despite the ramrod back and the aristocratic demeanour that make him seem so self-assured and somewhat grand and forbidding, he is a shy, sensitive man, painfully aware of and much inclined to exaggerate his own shortcomings. When I first met him he came to record the narration for a *son et lumière* production I was producing. His reading was impeccable, his instinctive phrasing flawless, the shading exactly what was required, but Sir John was deeply self-critical. 'I'm afraid I'm letting you down badly,' he kept saying. 'We'd better start all over again. Do please forgive me. I'm so sorry.'

However self-deprecating he may be at times, and whatever the public and critical reaction to his performances, Gielgud's overall attitude to his work is and always has been one of total dedication. The theatre is his life. His sense of commitment to it is absolute. While delighted by the success he has enjoyed in the cinema in his sixties and seventies, he has always found the business of film-making frustrating, rather resenting the early starts, the hanging around for hours waiting to do one three-minute take, the shooting out of sequence, the lack of real rehearsal, the fact, above all, that film is the director's and not the actor's medium. Over the past two decades he has grown to like working in the cinema more, but the theatre has always been and will always be his first love. It is when he is in a theatre that he is at his happiest and most relaxed. In 1973, I was responsible for the gala performance marking the golden jubilee of the Oxford Playhouse. Naturally Sir John, who had known his first real success as an actor with the Playhouse company in 1924/25, was top of the bill. He was to recite one speech from *Richard II* and I assumed would arrive at the theatre no more than an hour or two before the performance. In fact, he arrived first thing in the morning and sat in the stalls all day long engrossed in the work of the other actors rehearsing on stage, offering effusive words of encouragement and occasional, very tentative, words of advice.

Unlike some other fine players in the older actor-manager tradition, Gielgud has always sought to surround himself with the best. His pursuit of excellence is obsessive and his aim has always been to achieve success for a production as a whole rather than for himself as an individual. Many of his admirers claim that all too often, when directing a play in which he has also been starring, his concern for the production overall has been at the expense of his own performance. In a business not noted for those qualities, Gielgud is neither a selfish actor nor a jealous one. His generosity to other actors, especially those in whom he discerns real quality, is something I have been told about time and again while preparing this book. For example, a few years ago when Martin Jarvis played the title role in *Richard of Bordeaux* on the radio – a role Gielgud had created in 1932 and made totally his own – Sir John, who had never met him, wrote to the young actor out of the blue:

Dear Martin Jarvis,

Congratulations on your splendid performance in *Bordeaux* which I listened to last night with the keenest pleasure. The whole play came over faultlessly and the version and all the performances seemed just right – and knowing the whole thing by heart and having spent about two years of my life playing it, you can imagine I was hard to please.

I wish you might have the opportunity of giving it in the theatre for it seemed to me to hold up wonderfully well – and I believe the authoress would have been as satisfied as I, especially with your own performance.

All good wishes,
                Most sincerely,
                            John Gielgud

Generous and kind as Gielgud undoubtedly is, he can also be wonderfully tactless. He is famous for his *faux pas*, unintentionally hurtful remarks inadvertently blurted out at the most inappropriate moment, and of the countless stories of notorious 'Gielgud gaffes', some true, many, of course, apocryphal, my favourite is one recorded by Peter Ustinov in which Sir John managed to insult not just one poor individual but an entire nation! Let Mr Ustinov tell the story: 'I once saw him on a local late-night television interview in Saint Louis, Missouri. He was busy playing *The Ages of Man*, his one-man show, in half a ball-park, and now he was being interviewed by a long-winded intellectual.

'"One final question," the interviewer said. "Sir . . . Sir Gielgud . . . did you . . . oh, you must have had . . . we all did . . . at the start of your very wonderful . . . very wonderful and very meaningful . . . let me put it this way . . . did you have someone . . . a man . . . or . . . indeed, a woman . . . at whom you could point a finger and say . . . Yes! . . . This person helped me when I . . ."

'By now John understood what was being asked of him, and he prepared to answer, disguising his dislike of all that is pretentious by perfect courtesy.

'"Yes, I think there was somebody who taught me a great deal at my dramatic school, and I certainly am grateful to him for his kindness and consideration toward me. His name was Claude Rains."

'And then, as an afterthought, he added – "I don't know what happened to him. I think he failed, and went to America."'

If innocently I have perpetrated any ghastly gaffes in the pages that follow I hope Sir John will forgive me. What I have tried to do is provide a straightforward account of a remarkable and tumultuously crowded career, wherever possible using the words of eye-witnesses – Gielgud himself, his contemporaries, the critics who saw him most in action – and illustrating as many of his performances as space would allow. At about the time he took the photograph that faces this introduction, Cecil Beaton noted in his diary: 'In appearance John Gielgud looks, at first glance, anything but an artist. But, by degrees, one senses his poetic quality, his innate pathos. The large bulbous nose is a stage asset: the eyes, though tired, have a watery blue wistfulness that is in the Terry tradition of beauty. He is not altogether happy that he has inherited so many family characteristics, and praise of his mellifluous voice and superb diction embarrasses him. With the good manners that come from his true spirit, and not only on the stage, he has the grand manner. Unlike his rivals he does not know the sensation of jealousy; he will always plan to do the best for the project as a whole, rather than as a means of shining brightly himself. This has often led him to him playing small and ineffective roles, and even obliging someone else by doing the wrong thing for himself; however, in his case the 'wrong thing' only adds to his reputation for his innate devotion to the cause of the theatre.'

That innate devotion is what lies behind the unique life that this pictorial tribute to Sir John is designed to celebrate.

Arthur John Gielgud

John Gielgud was born in Kensington in London on 14 April, 1904. His father, Frank Gielgud, was a successful stockbroker, very much the comfortable Edwardian, despite the fact that he was of Lithuanian descent and only a second generation Londoner. Frank's father was born in England, and worked at the War Office and as a foreign correspondent, but his grandparents were Polish. One of Frank's grandmothers was an acclaimed Polish actress called Aniela Aszpergerowa. One of his grandfathers was a Polish cavalry officer called John Gielgud and it was this John Gielgud who left Poland for England in the 1830s.

The present John Gielgud's actual first name is Arthur. He was named after his maternal grandfather, Arthur Lewis, but the Arthur was soon dropped in favour of his second name and he was known as John or Jack to his family from an early age. His mother, Kate, belonged to one of the most distinguished of all theatrical clans: the Terrys. Her immediate family included at least twenty individuals closely concerned with the theatre, of whom the best known were probably her mother, Kate Terry, her uncle, Fred Terry, her aunt, Ellen Terry, and her cousins Gordon Craig and Phyllis Neilson-Terry.

John Gielgud in 1907.

Naturally, young John was delighted with his celebrated relations: 'I was enormously englamoured by my family, particularly the ones who were still acting when I was a boy. My parents didn't encourage this very much, although they were naturally very proud of it too. My mother was the theatrical one because she was a Terry; but my father, who was partly Polish, had a curious, practical, middle-class English realism, mixed with a certain romantic *panache*.'

John was the third of Kate and Frank Gielgud's four children, all of whom were 'tremendously theatrically minded'. They spent hours dressing up and playing acting games and their toy theatre – with a most ambitious and imaginative repertoire of home-made plays glorying in such titles as *Plots in the Harem*, *Lady Fawcett's Ruby* and *Kill That Spy* – absorbed and entertained them for much of their childhood.

John's formal education began when he followed his older brothers Lewis and Val to Hillside, a prep school in Godalming, where his academic career was not especially distinguished but where he was able to make his dramatic debut before a real audience. His first public performance was in the role of the Mock Turtle in a school production of *Alice in Wonderland*. 'I sang "Soup of the Evening" with increasing volume and shrillness in each verse.' Having given the Hillside boys, parents and teachers his Mock Turtle, he followed it up with his Humpty Dumpty, his Shylock and his Mark Antony. And when not starring in the works of Lewis Carroll and William Shakespeare, Gielgud Minor was engrossed in Ellen Terry's memoirs and the *Daily Sketch* reports of the theatrical garden parties of the day.

At the age of ten John certainly didn't know that he wanted to become an actor, but he knew he loved the theatre. If he had any particular ambition as a child it was possibly to follow in the footsteps of his cousin Gordon Craig and become a designer. But his parents had more straightforward ambitions for their son. Lewis was at Eton and John would have followed him there had he won the necessary scholarship. Val was at Rugby, but John failed to get the scholarship there as well. Instead he went to Westminster, where he didn't shine, but was happy enough and resolutely maintained his enthusiasm for all things theatrical.

The first play John was taken to was *Peter Pan* when he was seven. A year or so later he went to see his first Shakespeare, *As You Like It* at the Coronet Theatre, Notting Hill Gate, starring the great actor-manager Sir Frank Benson. As often as he was able he would go to the theatre and later to the music hall to see 'the greats'. He saw Sarah Bernhardt and Eleonora Duse and, of course, Ellen Terry. He saw Adeline Genée dance and heard Marie Lloyd and Vesta Tilley sing.

And when he wasn't at the theatre or reading about the theatre, he was enjoying his own amateur theatricals. All the young Gielguds – the three boys and their younger sister Eleanor – were enthusiastic actors, but John was the most devoted to the cause. Of these early amateur productions the one he remembered best marked his debut as Orlando in *As You Like It*. The play was per-

formed in the open air in a rectory garden at St Leonards-on-Sea. By his own admission, John was a somewhat vain young man. 'I affected very light grey flannels braced much too high, silk socks, broad-brimmed black soft hats, and even, I blush to admit, an eye-glass upon occasion, and I wore my hair very long and washed it a great deal to make it look fluffy and romantic. For Orlando, I slipped off to a hairdresser in St Leonards and asked the man to wave it – "For a play", I added hastily. "Certainly, sir," he said. "I suppose you'd be in the Pierrot Company that's opening on the Pier this week." Undaunted, I strode on to the lawn at the first performance, drew my sword fiercely, and declaimed: "Forbear, and eat no more!", but unfortunately I tripped over a large log and fell flat on my face. This was only the beginning of my troubles, for in the last act, when I pointed to the path where I was expecting Rosalind, with "Ah, here comes my Ganymede" – no Ganymede was to be seen. I said the line again, with a little less confidence this time; still no one appeared. I looked helplessly round, to find the prompter, his hands to his mouth, whispering as loudly as he dared across the hundred yards that separated us, "She's changed back into her girl's clothes a scene too soon!"'

It was at about the time of this inauspicious Orlando that John told his parents of his desire to go onto the stage. They had hoped that he might try for an Oxford scholarship, but having extracted an undertaking from him that should he not have had some measure of success as an actor by the age of twenty-five he would give it up and train to become an architect, reluctantly they

John Gielgud, third from the right, as Mark Antony in the Hillside School production of Julius Caesar.

allowed their stage-struck son to leave Westminster and enter for a scholarship at Lady Benson's dramatic school in the Cromwell Road.

This scholarship he won. His parents may not have been overjoyed, but his Terry grandmother was delighted.

Dear Old Jack,

I am delighted to hear of your intended real start in a profession you love, and wish you every success. You must not anticipate a bed of roses, for on the stage as in every other profession there are 'rubs and arrows' to contend with. 'Be kind and affable to all your co-mates, but if possible be intimate with none of them.' This is a quotation of my parents' advice to me and I pass it on as I have proved it to be very sound. Theatrical intimacy breeds jealousy of a petty kind which is very disturbing. I hope you may have many chances with your various studies and prove yourself worthy.

I am returning on Monday and shall, I hope, have an opportunity to have a good old talk with you.

Meanwhile, my love and congratulations.

Your affectionate grandmother,

Kate Lewis

It was while he was at Lady Benson's, where, by his own account, he was regarded as 'a talented but conceited pupil', that he made his first appearance at the Old Vic. Having heard that drama students were sometimes engaged as unpaid walk-ons there, he made his way to the celebrated theatre in the Waterloo Road and, at the age of seventeen, found himself cast as the Herald in Robert Atkins' production of *Henry V*. John only had one line – 'Here is the number of the slaughter'd French' – and no mention in the programme, but it was a start.

Henry V was in November 1921. In the following Spring John had three more walk-on parts at the Vic, in *Peer Gynt*, in *King Lear* and in a play by Halcott Glover about Wat Tyler. These weren't speaking roles, but they did earn John a mention in the programme where he was listed as 'Mr Giulgud'.

When his year at Lady Benson's was up, nepotism secured him his first proper job. His second cousin Phyllis Neilson-Terry offered him four pounds a week to play a few lines, understudy and be an assistant stage manager in a touring production of a play by J. B. Fagan called *The Wheel*. The tour opened in Bradford – to the incurably theatrical young Gielgud a wonderfully romantic city because Henry Irving had died there! – and took in the usual range of not-altogether glamorous dates in the North and the Midlands. During their week in Oxford one of the other members of

A wonderful play - almost realized. *Russell Thorndike remarkable fine and clever. I am very glad to have taken part in it.* 1922

OLD VIC.

The Royal Victoria Hall
Founded by the late Miss EMMA CONS in 1880.
OPPOSITE WATERLOO STATION, S.E.1.

Lessee and Manager ... ... LILIAN BAYLIS

Phone: HOP 1290.

PROGRAMME

10 PRODUCTIONS OF
IBSEN'S

PEER GYNT

With Grieg's Music and The Vic. Wagner Orchestra.

March 6, 8, 10, 13, 15, 17, at 7.30
Thursday 9, 16, at 2.   Saturday, 11, at 2.30
Easter Saturday, April 15, at 2.30 and 7.30

Produced by ROBERT ATKINS, and played by the "VIC." SHAKESPEARE COMPANY.

PROGRAMME—PRICE TWOPENCE.

PROGRAMME.

[PE]ER GYNT

A Dramatic Poem,
[B]Y HENRIK IBSEN

Translated by WILLIAM and CHARLES ARCHER.

...hunter charged by the author with most of the shortcomings of the race, especially with sloth and ...and awakens to find no core of reality in him, and he—who was always *sufficient* to himself, is startled ...der's mass with all the unsuccessful creatures, because he has never been *himself*. Yet he must go, unless ...amed, a woman's faithful love.

...gmented, will play Grieg's Music adapted by and under the direction of CHARLES CORRI.

[RU]SSELL THORNDIKE	The Captain of a Norwegian Ship ... ... ERNEST MEADS
[F]LORENCE BUCKTON	The Look Out ... ... HENRY COHEN
WILFRID WALTER	The Mate ... ... FRANCIS SULLIVAN
MAXWELL WRAY	The Cook ... ... HILTON EDWARDS
ERNEST MEADS	The Cabin Boy ... ... JOYCE CORNISH
NANCY HARKER	The Strange Passenger ... ... AUSTIN TREVOR
STELLA FRISTON	The Button Moulder ... ... RUPERT HARVEY
REYNER BARTON	
JOYCE CATHIE	Peasants, Trolls, Troll Imps, Dancing Girls, etc.:—
IRIS ROBERTS	Messrs. GIELGUD, GREEN, RILEY, PRIME, HUTCHISON,
AUSTIN TREVOR	Mesdames ROBSON, CLARKE, MYER, CORNISH, HAINES,
GLADYS DALE	ASHTON, BOYCE, WILLIAMS, BAXTER.
[ESTH]ER WHITEHOUSE	The Play has been arranged in Three Parts.
JANE BACON	Part I. ... GUDBRANDSDALE AND ON THE MOUNTAINS AROUND.
MARY HAMILTON	
[FRA]NCES PETERSEN	Part II. ... THE NORTH COAST OF AFRICA
ANDREW LEIGH	
D. HAY PETRIE	Part III. ... GUDBRANDSDALE AND ON THE MOUNTAINS AROUND.
AGNES CARTER	
[CATH]ERINE O'DWYER	The Management are indebted to William Archer, Esq., who has kindly lent the translation.
[WI]LFRID WALTER	
JOHN GARSIDE	Dances arranged by DAPHNE JAY, of the Mayfair School of Dancing.
AUSTIN TREVOR	Production by ROBERT ATKINS, and Executed by
[R]EYNER BARTON	WILFRID WALTER and HUBERT HINE.
[TH]AS HUTCHISON	
[MAR]Y MARTINEAU	Stage Manager ... ... HUBERT HINE
[NOR]TON EDWARDS	Assistant Stage Manager ... ... MAXWELL WRAY
[FRA]NCIS SULLIVAN	Stage Carpenter ... ... ROWLAND ROBINSON
ALAN WATTS	
[A]LTHEA GLASBY	

Opposite: Gielgud's second appearance at the Old Vic was in March 1922 as a walk-on in Peer Gynt, *directed by Robert Atkins, with Russell Thorndike, Sybil's younger brother, in the title part. Despite having his name misspelt in the programme, John relished the experience and noted on his copy of the programme: 'A wonderful play – almost realized. Russell Thorndike is remarkably fine and clever. I am very glad to have taken part in it.'*

the company, Alexander Sarner, suggested to John that one year at drama school wasn't enough: John was only eighteen and if he could get any more training he should.

John took Sarner's advice to heart and, when the tour was over, presented himself at the Royal Academy of Dramatic Art in Gower Street and managed to win himself another scholarship. He did well at RADA – where his contemporaries included Robert Harris, Beatrix Lehmann, Veronica Turleigh, Mervyn Johns, and George Howe who was to become a close friend and colleague over the years – and by the end of the first term he had secured himself his second proper professional engagement. John's mother happened to know Nigel Playfair, who came to see John in the end-of-term production of Barrie's *The Admirable Crichton*, and immediately offered him the part of Felix, the Poet Butterfly, in *The Insect Play* by Karel Capek, a somewhat 'modern' piece that viewed humanity in terms of insects. The cast also included Angela Baddeley, Elsa Lanchester and John's favourite teacher from RADA, Claude Rains, but the play was a flop and John felt ineffective and even embarrassed in his part.

The Insect Play: *Gielgud as the Poet Butterfly at the Regent Theatre, May 1923. This picture never appealed to John: 'Looking at it, I am surprised that the audience didn't throw things at me . . . I wore white flannels, pumps, a silk shirt, a green laurel-wreath, fair hair, and a golden battledore and shuttlecock . . . The Insect Play was a failure and I created a very bad impression in it.'*

Felix Aylmer, John Gielgud, Claude Rains and Tristan Rawson in Robert E. Lee *at the Regent Theatre, June 1923.*

Playfair's next venture at the Regent Theatre was more successful. It was *Robert E. Lee* by the poet John Drinkwater, directed by Playfair and the author and featuring most of the company from *The Insect Play*. John was relieved and grateful to be retained, the more so because while appearing in the play in the evening he was able to complete his studies at RADA during the day.

At the end of 1923, his RADA training behind him, he managed to get himself cast as Charley in a Christmas revival of Brandon Thomas's classic farce *Charley's Aunt*, which played twice daily at the Comedy Theatre for six weeks. It was useful experience, physically exhausting if not altogether demanding. Even more useful and certainly much more taxing was his next engagement.

In 1923, J. B. Fagan, an Ulsterman and actor turned playwright and producer, founded the Oxford Playhouse in a disused big game museum in the Woodstock Road in Oxford and invited John to join the company. Fagan wanted to establish a serious repertory theatre in Oxford and launched his venture with an ambitious first season and a remarkable team of young actors that included Flora Robson, Tyrone Guthrie, Raymond Massey and Richard Goolden. Between January 1924 and August 1925 John appeared in a total of eighteen different productions at the Oxford Playhouse. He played a wide variety of roles in plays by Goldsmith and Congreve, by Shaw and J. M Synge, by A. A. Milne and Somerset Maugham, by Chekhov and Ibsen and Maeterlinck and Pirandello, but in none by Shakespeare.

AN APPEAL.

THE breach between literature and the stage which the modern commercial theatre in this country does little to remedy is a matter of concern to all who are interested in dramatic literature.

It appears to us only right that Oxford should encourage the efforts which are being made sporadically by individuals to raise the standard of the acted drama in England,—the only great country in the world where neither Government nor Municipality will move a finger to support the most democratic of the arts.

A seven years' lease of The Playhouse during term time has been secured. Works by dramatists, living or dead, such as fall within the category of dramatic literature will form the programmes of future seasons, and the selection being in the hands of the players they may be relied on to present plays suited to the stage rather than to the study, and providing scope for the art of acting.

The success or failure of this interesting adventure lies in the hands of the Members of the University and the Citizens of Oxford, and we confidently appeal to them to support a movement which promises to supply Oxford with a distinguished source of entertainment, and to assist in raising the theatre to the position which it has occupied in the great cultural epochs of the past.

(Signed)

J. M. BARRIE.
ARNOLD BENNETT.
ARTHUR BOURCHIER.
ROBERT BRIDGES.
W. L. COURTNEY.
CURZON.
EDWARD ELGAR.
J. B. FAGAN.
JOHN GALSWORTHY.
FRANK GRAY (M.P. for Oxford).
THOMAS HARDY.
HENRY ARTHUR JONES.

(Signed)

JOHN LAVERY.
JOHN MASEFIELD.
LILLAH McCARTHY.
A. A. MILNE.
GILBERT MURRAY.
ARTHUR PINERO.
NIGEL PLAYFAIR.
BERNARD SHAW.
CLIVE SHIELDS (Pres. O.U.D.S.).
TOM BASSON (Mayor of Oxford).
ALFRED SUTRO.

Evenings at 8.10.   Matinee, Thursday 2.15.

LOVE FOR LOVE

BY

WILLIAM CONGREVE.

SIR SAMPSON LEGEND, father of Valentine and Ben ...	REGINALD DENHAM.
VALENTINE, fallen under his father's displeasure by his expensive way of living, in love with Angelica ...	JOHN GIELGUD.
SCANDAL, his friend, a free speaker	PETER CRESWELL.
TATTLE, a half witted beau, vain of his amours yet valuing himself for secrecy	EARLE GREY.
BEN, Sir Sampson's younger son, half home-bred and half sea-bred, designed to marry Miss Prue ...	R. S. SMITH.
FORESIGHT, an illiterate old fellow, peevish and positive, superstitious, and pretending to understand astrology, palmistry, physiognomy, omens, dreams, etc.; uncle to Angelica	RICHARD GOOLDEN.
JEREMY, servant to Valentine	W. T. GUTHRIE.
TRAPLAND, a scrivener	HERBERT LUGG.
BUCKRAM, a lawyer	HERBERT LUGG.
ANGELICA, neice to Foresight, of a considerable fortune in her hands	FLORA ROBSON.
MRS. FORESIGHT, second wife of Foresight	MOLLY McARTHUR.
MRS. FRAIL, sister to Mrs. Foresight, a woman of the town	MARY GREY.
MISS PRUE, a daughter of Foresight by a former wife, a silly awkward country girl	JANE ELLIS.
NURSE to Miss Prue	BERTHA PHILIPS.

Scene   -   LONDON.

Acts I and III in Valentine's Lodgings.   Acts II and IV in Foresight's House.

Play Produced by REGINALD DENHAM.

STAGE MANAGERS ... ... { W. T. GUTHRIE.
                                   { HERBERT LUGG.

Wigs by CLARKSON.

Costumes by NATHAN.

Furniture supplied by WALFORD & SPOKES, } High Street,
THE ANTIQUARY, } Oxford.
GREENINGS, }

Buses leave for North and East Oxford after each performance.

The Presentational Stage designed by J. B. FAGAN.

Gielgud joined the new Oxford Playhouse company in January 1924 and appeared in a total of eighteen different productions: 'The biggest success of the first season was Love for Love which shocked North Oxford and a lot of our regular patrons, but delighted a large section of the University, and drew many people to the Playhouse for the first time, chiefly I am afraid, on account of its scandalous dialogue and improper situations.'

THE
OXFORD
PLAYHOUSE
WOODSTOCK RD.   PROPRIETOR. F. H. BALLARD.

Lessee ... ...

By permission of the Vice-Chancellor and the Right Worshipful the Mayor.

ARTHUR PYKE.

On MONDAY, JANUARY 28th, at 8.10.

THE OXFORD PLAYERS

IN

Love for Love

BY

WILLIAM CONGREVE.

For Six Nights, and Thursday Matinee at 2.15.

2d.

Next Week— "MR. PIM PASSES BY."
Fourth Week— No performances.
Fifth Week— "SHE STOOPS TO CONQUER."
Sixth Week— "MONNA VANNA."
Seventh Week—"THE LAND OF HEART'S DESIRE" and "THE MAN OF DESTINY."
Eighth Week— "THE ŒDIPUS OF SOPHOCLES."

Hon. Director   -   -   J. B. FAGAN.

However in 1924 John did manage to appear in *Romeo and Juliet* – twice. And both times it was in London. In February he played Paris and understudied the Romeo of Gyles Isham – Oxford's golden boy the early 1920s – in an amateur production staged at the RADA theatre. Then in April he received a most unusual letter.

Opposite: Romeo and Juliet *with Gwen Ffrangcon-Davies, aged twenty-eight, and John Gielgud, a few weeks after his twentieth birthday.*

2nd April 1924

Dear Mr Gielgud,
    If you would like to play the finest lead among the plays by the late William Shakespeare, will you please call upon Mr Peacock and Mr Ayliff at the Regent Theatre on Friday at 2.30 p.m. Here is an opportunity to become a London Star in a night.
                Please confirm.
                    Yours very truly,
                    Akerman May

It transpired that Barry Jackson was planning to put on *Romeo and Juliet* at the Regent Theatre, to be directed by H. K. Ayliff, with Gwen Ffrangcon-Davies as Juliet, and they wanted John for Romeo. He leapt at the opportunity, naturally yearning for a triumph, but actually achieving what he later described as 'a pretty good disaster': 'I had the most terrible clothes, to begin with, and the most wickedly unbecoming wig. . . . I didn't know how to move. I think I spoke not badly; but we had a very, very drastic director; and I just wasn't ready. I didn't know how to select what I wanted to do, or put over emotion. I just enjoyed indulging in my own emotions, and imagined that that was acting. I only learnt, long afterwards, that you may indulge your emotions in imagining a part, but you mustn't allow them free rein until you have selected exactly what you want to show the audience, and how much you should show while you're doing it.'

Ayliff was a hard task-master and not easily satisfied. The cast were forced to play the dress rehearsal with the safety curtain down because Jackson had invited an audience and Ayliff thought the play wasn't ready for one. When it did open the critical reception was mixed for the company in general and poor for John in particular: 'unduly consumptive', 'niminy piminy', 'scant of virility'. Ivor Brown pronounced: 'Mr Gielgud has the most meaningless legs imaginable.' Indeed John had been painfully aware of his awkward gait and mannered posturing ever since Lady Benson had told him he walked like 'a cat with rickets'. It took him years to gain full command over his physical movements and appearance on stage: 'As a young actor I pranced and was very self-conscious. Then I became too graceful and posed. Now that I am less shy and able to study myself with more detachment, I have tried to control my physical mannerisms by observing them and asking to have them checked by others, which I was originally too vain and shy to do.'

Above: The Seagull; *Randolph McLeod (standing left) as Trigorin, Valerie Taylor (centre) as Nina, and John Gielgud (standing right) as Konstantin at the Little Theatre, October 1925.*

Left: The Three Sisters; *John Gielgud as Tusenbach and Beatrix Thomson as Irina at the Barnes Theatre, February 1926.*

JOHN GIELGUD.
IN
"THE SEAGULL".

After the disappointment of Romeo in London, John was glad to get back to Oxford where on the whole his work was being rather better received and where happily he achieved his first notable success as Trofimov in *The Cherry Orchard*. 'It was the first time I ever went on stage and felt that perhaps I could really act'.

Chekhov was still a relatively unknown quantity as far as British audiences were concerned and J. B. Fagan's production caused quite a stir. Nigel Playfair came to Oxford, admired it and invited Fagan to bring it to London, where it played first at Playfair's theatre, the Lyric, Hammersmith, and then moved on to the Royalty. In London the play was given a schizophrenic reception. Some critics were vituperative. A few were bewildered. Most were enthusiastic. One or two were ecstatic. In the *Sunday Times* James Agate, doyen of British drama critics, was unequivocal: 'I suggest that *The Cherry Orchard* is one of the great plays of the world.' He was equally generous about the performance of Trofimov: 'perfection itself', he called it.

The overall success of *The Cherry Orchard* inspired Philip Ridgeway, a Northern impresario and a comparative newcomer to London, to attempt to mount a complete 'Chekhov Season' with productions of *The Seagull*, *The Three Sisters*, *Ivanov* and *Uncle Vanya*, and he invited John to join the company. *The Seagull* was directed by A. E. Filmer. John played Konstantin, 'a very romantic character, a sort of miniature Hamlet', and received favourable notices from the press, but severe criticism from several of his friends who found his movements mannered and his diction affected. The play was a success at the Little Theatre in 1925, but when four years later it was revived briefly at the Arts, John was disappointed in both the production and his performance. He was anxious to make changes, but A. E. Filmer wanted to leave well alone: 'What a pity you always want to gild the lily.'

Philip Ridgeway followed up *The Seagull* with his second Chekhov, *The Three Sisters*, presented at a tiny theatre he was leasing out at Barnes. For this production he had engaged the legendary Russian director and disciple of Stanislavsky, Theodore Komisarjevsky, known to friends and colleagues as Komis. Despite the fact that Komis deliberately distorted the nature of Tusenbach, making him handsome rather than plain and forcing John to play against the grain of the part, the play was well received. But its success notwithstanding, the rest of the Chekhov season didn't materialise. Komis did direct one more Russian play for Philip Ridgeway and John played in it, but it wasn't *Ivanov*. It was *Katerina* by Andreyev in which John played a betrayed middle-aged husband, 'a sort of Slavonic Othello', and felt he cut quite a dash. James Agate agreed – with reservations. 'Mr Gielgud is becoming one of our most admirable actors: there is mind behind everything he does. Only he must avoid the snag of portentousness, of being intense about nothing in particular.'

Komis was an eccentric and not always comfortable director, but over the next ten years John worked with him in four more productions and found him both stimulating and helpful. In 1963 when Gielgud came to write *Stage Directions*, his book about the art and craft of the theatre, he acknowledged his debt to Komis for 'teaching me not to act from outside, seizing on obvious effects and histrionics; to avoid the temptations of showing off; to work from within to present a character, and to absorb the atmosphere and general background of a play ... He also gave me my first important lesson in trying to act with relaxation – the secret of all good acting.'

In 1925, when *The Cherry Orchard* had finished its run at the Oxford Playhouse in January and before it opened in May at the Lyric, Hammersmith, John, thanks in part to his ability to play the piano a bit (a gift he claims to have inherited from his father), got the chance to understudy Noël Coward in his controversial drama *The Vortex*. He understudied Coward in the part at the Royalty, the Comedy and the Little Theatre, and actually went on for him on three nerve-wracking occasions, before taking over the part for the final four weeks of the run. A year later he took over from Coward again and played Lewis Dodd in the stage version of Margaret Kennedy's romantic best-seller *The Constant Nymph*. It was John's first leading role in a West End hit and his

Above: (and cartoon) with Mrs. Patrick Campbell in Ghosts, *1928 and left: as Lewis Dodd in* The Constant Nymph, *1926.*

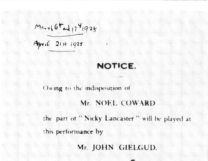

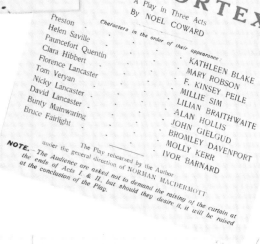

NOTICE.

Owing to the indisposition of

Mr. NOEL COWARD

the part of "Nicky Lancaster" will be played at

this performance by

Mr. JOHN GIELGUD.

LITTLE THEATRE
JOHN STREET, ADELPHI, STRAND

Every Evening at 8.40
Matinees Tuesday, Wednesday and Friday at 2.30

NORMAN MACDERMOTT
PRESENTS
THE EVERYMAN THEATRE COMPANY IN

THE VORTEX

A Play in Three Acts
By NOEL COWARD

Characters in the order of their appearance:

Preston	KATHLEEN BLAKE
Helen Saville	MARY ROBSON
Pauncefort Quentin	F. KINSEY PEILE
Clara Hibbert	MILLIE SIM
Florence Lancaster	LILIAN BRAITHWAITE
Tom Veryan	ALAN HOLLIS
Nicky Lancaster	JOHN GIELGUD
David Lancaster	BROMLEY DAVENPORT
Bunty Mainwaring	MOLLY KERR
Bruce Fairlight	IVOR BARNARD

The Play rehearsed by the Author under the general direction of NORMAN MACDERMOTT

NOTE. The Audience are asked not to demand the raising of the curtain at the ends of Acts I. & II., but should they desire it, it will be raised at the conclusion of the Play.

Right: understudying and taking over from Noël Coward in The Vortex, *1925.*

Below: Gielgud's photograph featured for the first time in a theatre programme when he appeared as Captain Allenby in The Skull, *1928.*

John Gielgud

"The Skull"

John Deverell

SHAFTESBURY
THEATRE

The
DANIEL MAYER COMPANY
PRESENT

"THE SKULL"

A
COMEDY MYSTERY THRILLER
in Three Acts

by

BERNARD J. McOWEN
and
HARRY E. HUMPHREY

6d.

first taste of a long run. 'I found it terribly irksome. The part was extremely tiring, and I had a bad time because the company didn't like me very much. They resented Noël leaving and I wasn't very happy with the direction that I got, such as it was. But the play was an enormous success and I learned the hard way, how to carry this very long and exhausting part for more than a year and afterwards for quite a long tour.'

While he was appearing in *The Constant Nymph* John did as he had done since he began his career as a professional actor and appeared regularly in one-off Sunday performances and special matinees of a wide variety of other plays. At the Savoy, for example, he appeared as Ferdinand in a few performances of *The Tempest*. At the Apollo he played Cassio in a special performance of *Othello*. At Wyndham's he appeared with Mrs Patrick Campbell in *Ghosts* for a series of special matinees marking the Ibsen centenary.

When the tour of *The Constant Nymph* was over, John set off for New York and his Broadway debut as the Tsarevitch Alexander in Alfred Neumann's *The Patriot*. The play was a flop and John had hardly disembarked from the S.S. *Berlin* that had taken him to New York before he was setting sail for London again. During the next eighteen months he appeared in ten different plays in London. None was a notable success. 'They were terrible plays, but I took everything that was offered to me, pretty well. I was the leading man, which was a new experience for me; I was getting good billing and a good salary; so I thought that perhaps acting was just being in work and doing whatever came along.'

John was now twenty-five and a busy working actor with a bit of a name and something of a reputation. At least he didn't have to throw in his hand and become an architect.

'I'm a star'

Lilian Baylis, founder of the Old Vic and Sadler's Wells companies, was one of the most unlikely and influential figures in the history of the British theatre. Born in 1874 she went with her family to South Africa at the age of sixteen and embarked there on a musical career which was interrupted in 1895 when she returned to London to help her aunt, Emma Cons, run the Victoria Theatre opposite Waterloo Station as a temperance hall known as the Royal Victorian Coffee Musical Hall. When Emma Cons died in 1912, Miss Baylis took over the management and began to transform the theatre into what was to become the legendary Old Vic: a place where drama and opera of real quality could be brought to ordinary people. Between 1914 and 1923 *all* of Shakespeare's plays were performed at the Old Vic and when

When Gielgud joined the Old Vic in 1929 the company produced postcard portraits of the their twenty-five-year-old star attraction.

Previous page: Complete with autograph, the very first 'fan photograph' of the rising Shakespearean star.

John Gielgud as Mark Antony, Harcourt Williams as Brutus and Donald Wolfit as Cassius in Julius Caesar, *1930.*

drama threatened to overwhelm opera in the theatre's programme, she took over, rebuilt and in 1931 opened the Sadler's Wells Theatre as a home for opera and ballet. Single-minded, determined, intensely religious, with the manner of a shuffling landlady rather than a pervader of art for the masses, Miss Baylis was a formidable individual who succeeded against all the odds and managed to maintain the most remarkable artistic standards despite continuous financial hardship. Her secretary is said once to have looked into her office and found Miss Baylis on her knees and at prayer: 'Dear God, send me a good Hamlet – but make him cheap.'

In 1929 Lilian Baylis engaged Harcourt Williams as her producer at the Old Vic. Williams was then almost fifty, an established actor who had appeared with many of the 'greats': Ellen Terry, Frank Benson, George Alexander, Martin Harvey and John Barrymore. He came to the Vic with a nascent reputation as an innovator that grew considerably during his five years with the company. Something of an intellectual as well as being a seasoned performer, an ardent admirer of Gordon Craig and a devoted student of Harley Granville-Barker's *Prefaces to Shakespeare*, his productions were initially reviled then gradually acclaimed as landmarks in the history of Shakespearean presentation.

When he came to the Vic, Harcourt Williams had no doubt that the two figures he wanted to lead the company were John Gielgud and Martita Hunt. After protracted negotiations – Miss Baylis took her usual line: 'We can't afford stars' – he secured the services of both of them and John moved south of the Thames to begin one of the most exciting and rewarding phases of his career.

Gielgud stayed with the Vic Company for just two seasons, but in the twenty months between September 1929 and April 1931 he played the whole gamut of Shakespeare's leading men: Romeo, Richard II, Oberon, Mark Antony, Orlando, Macbeth, Hamlet, Hotspur, Prospero, Antony, Malvolio, Benedick and Lear! He also took on Antonio in *The Merchant of Venice*, Cléante in Molière's *The Imaginary Invalid*, the title role in Pirandello's *The Man With a Flower in his Mouth*, Lord Trinket in George Colman's 1761 comedy *The Jealous Wife*, and, since Harcourt Williams was an enthusiastic Shavian, the Emperor in *Androcles and the Lion* and Sergius in *Arms and the Man*.

John's first performance was as Romeo. Adele Dixon played Juliet, Martita Hunt the Nurse, Gyles Isham was Mercutio and the company included Donald Wolfit as Tybalt. The production was not a success, as Wolfit later recollected: 'Almost everyone was blamed for taking the play at such a speed that the verse and poetry were entirely lost. The Prologue does indeed speak of

Opposite Richard II, *1929.*

Romeo and Juliet *with Adele Dixon, 1930.*

"the two hours' traffic of our stage" and we nearly achieved that.'
Even Harcourt Williams,who encouraged the playing of the verse
with speed and verve, was disappointed with Gielgud's Romeo.
'The least interesting performance of his two years at the Old Vic,'
he called it. 'He certainly gave little hint of the power to come,
albeit it was a thoughtful, well-graced performance, and he spoke
beautifully. But he never touched the last scenes. He failed to bring
off the distracted boy jolted by disaster into full manhood; the
ecstasy, too, of the last moments transcending death escaped him.'

Gielgud didn't achieve particular success at the Vic that season
until the fourth production, but then the success was a notable
one. Ever since seeing Ernest Milton's memorable *Richard II* at
the Vic in the 1920/21 Vic season, Gielgud had wanted to play
the part and now, in November 1929, and wearing Ernest
Milton's old costume, he seized his chance. It was an undoubted
personal triumph and many people felt that his interpretation of
the role was the spearhead of a new kind of acting. Talking about
it in restrospect some thirty years later, Gielgud disagreed: 'I think
it was more the result of an old kind of acting that I inherited
from the Terrys and what I call the *panache* actors I admired so
much in my youth: a certain gift of projection and an unreal kind
of romantic acting, which I did with so much conviction for myself
that I did manage to convince the audience. Richard is, after all,
a very affected and elaborately romantic, attitudinizing, part. But
now, when I listen to my old recordings, they sound to me very
voice-conscious, and I'm rather ashamed to think that I was so
contented with that kind of acting. I don't really believe it has
the truth in it that I would like, except, of course, that in *Richard II*
the man is meant to be studying himself and indulging in his own
sorrows, so that it may have been more appropriate.'

At the time Gielgud's Richard II was considered to have truth
and beauty. Ivor Brown called it 'exquisite'. Harcourt Williams
saw it as the turning-point in the season: 'His playing of the
Coronation scene will live in my mind as one of the great things
I have witnessed in the theatre. A tall, willowy figure in black
velvet, surmounted by a fair head, the pale agonized face set
beneath a glittering crown.'

In the Spring of 1930, when Gielgud had not yet turned twenty-
six, Harcourt Williams suggested to him that he might like to try
a real Shakespearean heavyweight and have a go at Macbeth.
Given Gielgud's age and physical appearance at the time, it was
unlikely casting, but now he was taking Shakespeare at the flood
and rose unhesitatingly to the challenge. Basing the look and feel
of his performance on what he had read and heard of Henry Irving's Macbeth, John achieved a surprising success in the part,
helped no doubt by a fine Lady Macbeth from Martita Hunt who
was herself only thirty. The rest of the company, the public and
the critics were equally impressed. James Agate declared: 'For the
first time in my experience Macbeth retained his hold upon the
play until the end.' And Ivor Brown exhorted his readers: 'See
Macbeth at the Old Vic and be able to tell your children that you
saw the great John Gielgud in his prime.'

Macbeth, *1930. 'My physical picture of Macbeth was derived principally from the drawings of Irving by Bernard Partridge which I had seen in a souvenir of the Lyceum production. I made up in the last act with whitened hair and bloodshot eyes, trying to resemble as nearly as I could "the gaunt famished wolf" of Ellen Terry's description of Irving.'*

The next peak that John was set to assault in that awe-inspiring season was *Hamlet*. When he had first met Lilian Baylis and discussed what parts he might play at the Vic she had teased him about the possiblity of Hamlet, suggesting that there were several young players in the company who might be equally fitted to take it on – Gyles Isham being one. In the event Isham played Horatio and Gielgud played Hamlet, with Adele Dixon as Ophelia, Martita Hunt as Gertrude and Donald Wolfit as Claudius. Tyrone Guthrie described it as 'a very youthful, thrilling Hamlet' and, although John was to play the part off and on for another fourteen years, he quickly recognized the advantage of playing it young. 'Hamlet had never been allowed to be given to a very young actor until I played it. . . . I don't think anybody (except Master Betty) had ever played it under thirty-five, and it made people realize the tragedy of the beginning of the play in a way that an older man can never achieve.'

The production – which included two performances of the complete text of the play, generally known to the cast as 'the Eternity Version' – provided a fitting climax to the season and was so successful that it secured for Miss Baylis her first West End transfer. In June the play opened at the Queen's Theatre in Shaftesbury Avenue and John received the best notices of his career: 'a great performance', 'a unique achievement', 'puts him beyond the range of arriving actors; he is in the first rank'. James Agate ran through his thesaurus of superlatives: 'This actor is young, thoughtful, clever, sensitive; his performance is subtle, brilliant, vigorous, imaginative, tender and full of the right kind of ironic humour . . . I have no hesitation in saying that it is the high water mark of English Shakespearean acting in our time.'

Gielgud's first Hamlet, 1930, with Donald Wolfit as Claudius. 'I threw myself into the part like a man learning to swim and I found the text would hold me up if I sought the truth in it.'

Agate was not nearly so enthusiastic about Gielgud's next venture. Between the end of the run of *Hamlet* at the Queen's and the start of the new Vic season in September, John made the first of his five appearances as John Worthing in *The Importance of Being Earnest*. This was under Sir Nigel Playfair's management at the Lyric, Hammersmith, and featured John's distinguished aunt, Mabel Terry Lewis, as a powerful Lady Bracknell. The public and most of the critics enjoyed the production and Gielgud clearly revelled in a part so very different from Hamlet yet one which, in the coming years, he was to make equally his own.

1930, The Importance of Being Earnest, *with Mabel Terry Lewis, as Lady Bracknell.*

At the beginning of the new season at the Old Vic, Ralph Richardson joined the company. He was a couple of years older than John and initially the two actors were wary of one another. When Sir Ralph died in the autumn of 1983 Gielgud recalled their first encounter: 'When we first acted together at the Old Vic in 1930, I little thought that we might be friends. At first we were inclined to circle round each other like suspicious dogs. In our opening production I played Hotspur to his Prince Hal, and was relieved, though somewhat surprised, to discover that he was as reluctant as I to engage in the swordplay demanded in the later under-rehearsed scenes at Shrewsbury. On the first night I was amazed at his whispered instructions – surely, I thought, the audience must hear them too – "Now you hit me, cocky. Now I hit you."

'A few weeks later, as we moved into rehearsals for *The Tempest*, I rather hesitatingly ventured to suggest to him a private session for examining one of our scenes together, and he immediately agreed with the greatest modesty and good humour. This was, as he has often said himself, the beginning of a friendship that was to last for fifty years.'

Opposite: Twelfth Night: *Harcourt Williams (extreme right) rehearses the Old Vic company for the special opening production of the Sadler's Wells Theatre under Lilian Baylis's management, January 1931.*

Making up for his debut as Prospero in The Tempest, *in October 1930. At Komisarjevsky's suggestion Gielgud didn't wear a beard for the part and made himself up to look like Dante.*

THE OPENING CEREMONY OF SADLER'S WELLS.

PROGRAMME

National Anthem. Conducted by Percy Pitt, a Governor of the Vic.
First verse sung by Joan Cross.
Second verse sung by Constance Willis.
Chorus by members, past and present, of the Vic Opera and Shakespeare Companies, and the audience.
In the Chair—The Mayor of Finsbury, Councillor C. R. Simpson, J.P., L.C.C. Supported by members of the Old Vic Governing Body, the Sadler's Wells Committee, Dame Madge Kendal, the Mayors of Hackney, Holborn, Islington, St. Pancras, Shoreditch, Stoke Newington, and representatives of The Carnegie U.K. Trust, and other public bodies which have helped the Fund.
Borough Welcome to Sadler's Wells Theatre by the Mayor of Finsbury.
Formal Declaration that the theatre is open by Sir Johnston Forbes-Robertson.
Mr. Rowe, Hon. Secretary and Treasurer of the Sadler's Wells Fund, to read a message from H.R.H. The Prince of Wales and others, and make a short financial statement.

TWELFTH NIGHT

(SHAKESPEARE)

Played by VIC SHAKESPEARE COMPANY.

Produced by HARCOURT WILLIAMS.

Characters in the order of their appearance:—

Orsino, *Duke of Illyria*	GODFREY KENTON
Curio	DAVID BALFOUR
Valentine *Gentlemen attending on the Duke*	ERIC PHILLIPS
Viola	DOROTHY GREEN
A Sea Captain	ALFRED SANGSTER
Sir Toby Belch, *kinsman to Olivia*	RALPH RICHARDSON
Maria, *Olivia's woman*	ELSA PALMER
Sir Andrew Aguecheek	GEORGE HOWE
Feste, *a clown*	LESLIE FRENCH
Olivia	JOAN HARBEN
Malvolio, *steward to Olivia*	JOHN GIELGUD
Antonio, *a sea captain*	HENRY WOLSTON
Sebastian, *brother to Viola*	ANTHONY HAWTREY
Fabian	RICHARD RIDDLE
A Priest	VALENTINE DYALL
First Officer	WILFRID GRANTHAM

Lords, Ladies, Sailors, Officers, etc.—Phillip Fothergill, Gordon Richardson, Harold Chapin, James Lytton, Cleeran Bell, Lyos Brown, Francis Brady, Doreen Purdie, Pamela Henry-May, Ethel Glendinning, Alexis France, Prudence Major, Doreen Barrington, Mary Humphreys, Phyllis Homfray, Ursula Martindale, Christine Malcery.

The Play will be given in Two Parts, with an interval of fifteen minutes.

The audience will greatly assist the atmosphere of the play if they will kindly remain silent after the lowering of the lights and refrain from striking matches during the progress of scenes. H.W.

Costumes and Settings designed and arranged by OWEN P. SMYTH.

Harpsichord by HENRY TULL (Chiswick).

The Music under the Direction of HERBERT MENGES.
The Song, "Come away Death," set by Christopher Wilson.

Acting Manager for Sadler's Wells	R. Noble
Lighting Effects and Stage Management	Michael Watts
Assistant Stage Managers	Margaret Mackenzie, Fabia Harcourt Smith
Press Representatives	L. E. Behrens, Dorothy Deare
Stage Carpenter	Rowland Robinson
Electrician (Vic)	Jack Ellis
Settings painted by	Leslie Young
Wardrobe Mistress	Mrs. Newman
Wardrobe Master	G. Whitehead

Dorothy Green dressed as Viola and John Gielgud dressed as Hotspur, with Lilian Baylis in January 1931.

King Lear: Gielgud's farewell to the Old Vic in April 1931. 'It was distinctly ambitious on me to dare, at the age of twenty-six, to try to assume "the large effects that troop with majesty" as eighty-year-old King Lear.'

November 1930, Antony and
Cleopatra *with Dorothy Green;*
February 1931, Sergius in
Arms and the Man.

As well as Prince Hal and Caliban, Richardson had a particular success that season with Sir Toby Belch (to Gielgud's Malvolio) and Bluntscli in *Arms and the Man* (to Gielgud's Sergius). The highspots for John in 1930/31 were a well-regarded Prospero in *The Tempest,* a solid Antony in *Antony and Cleopatra* and an entertaining and effective Benedick in *Much Ado about Nothing.* At the end of the season he was given the option of reviving his triumphant *Hamlet* or essaying *King Lear.* Characteristically he chose the new challenge and gave a performance as Lear that was by no means universally acclaimed, but was generally realized as showing the makings of a future Lear of greatness.

DAILY SKETCH

SATURDAY, NOVEMBER

Week-en

OLD VIC REVIVAL

Wearing costumes taken from Elizabethan models, John Gielgud and Dorothy Green in " Antony and Cleopatra " at the Old Vic on Monday.—(*Daily Sketch.*)

John's second season at the Vic may have lacked the epoch-making triumphs that characterized the first, but it broadened his range, sharpened his technique and helped further establish him as a major star. That year Harold Nicolson wrote in his diary, 'I think he may well be the finest actor we have had since Irving.' Most of his contemporaries would have concurred. Gielgud himself found the experience of playing so many major roles in such a limited space of time both exhausting and exhilarating. Being thrown in at the deep end, he was forced to react instinctively to the parts, not studying the details, but imagining the whole. Many years later he recalled: 'This happened to me with all the great parts I played when I was at the Vic as a young man – Lear, Macbeth, Antony, Hamlet. In some cases, particularly in *Macbeth*, I had more success the first time than when I came to study the part more thoroughly twelve years later. I simply imagined it, and acted it for the main development and broad lines

With Adele Dixon in The Good Companions *at His Majesty's, 1931. The part of Inigo Jollifant 'made very few demands' and Gielgud rehearsed it while he was still playing King Lear at the Old Vic.*

of the character, without worrying about the technical, intellectual, and psychological difficulties. I played it from scene to scene as it seemed to come to me as we rehearsed the play. With only three weeks, of course, there was not time to do much more than that. I think one should dare to fly high when one is young; one may sometimes surprise oneself. It is wonderful to be able to give the imagination full play, hardly realizing what an exciting danger is involved.'

After two seasons at the Old Vic, Gielgud was ready to get back to the West End and he returned to the commercial theatre in Edward Knoblock's stage version of J. B. Priestley's novel *The Good Companions*. It was a considerable popular success and gave John his longest run since *The Constant Nymph*. He was now a fully-fledged London star, with billing and salary to match. *The Good Companions* was followed by another long West End run in *Musical Chairs* by Ronald Mackenzie. Originally entitled *The Discontents*,

With Carol Goodner in Musical Chairs *at the Criterion, 1932.*

CRITERION
THEATRE
Licensed by the Lord Chamberlain to HOWARD WYNDHAM

"The clout you'll get some day"

Photo by Sasha

Lessees
THE WYNDHAM THEATRES, Ltd.
The New Theatre, St. Martin's Lane, W.C.

Managing Directors
HOWARD WYNDHAM and BRONSON ALBERY

the play had heavy Chekhovian overtones and Gielgud felt Komis would be the right director. The production was not without its traumas – Komis was often not in attendance – but when it opened it found general favour with critics and public alike and ran comfortably from April Fool's Day to New Year's Eve.

In 1932 Gielgud also made his debut as a director, producing the Oxford University Dramatic Society in *Romeo and Juliet* and persuading two notable professional actresses to lead the company of undergraduate amateurs. Peggy Ashcroft was Juliet and Edith Evans the Nurse. John had long wanted to try his hand as a director and once he got the taste for the craft he never lost it. Over the next two years he directed five West End shows – *Strange Orchestra* by Rodney Ackland at the St Martin's, *Sheppey* by Somerset Maugham at Wyndham's, *Spring 1600* by Emlyn Williams at the Shaftesbury, *Queen of Scots* by Gordon Daviot at the New, and Rodney Ackland's adaptation of Hugh Walpole's novel *The Old Ladies*, again at the New – as well as returning to the Old Vic to direct *The Merchant of Venice* for Harcourt Williams and going back to Oxford to direct the OUDS in *Richard II*.

'Richard of Bordeaux was a big stepping-stone in my career.' Gielgud tried out the play at the Arts Theatre in June 1932 and then produced it himself at the New Theatre in February 1933. 'I realised at once that Richard was a gift from heaven, and I felt sure that Gwen Ffrangcon-Davies would be exquisite as Anne.'

In the twenties he had appeared in a couple of unremarkable films. In 1932–35 he appeared in three more: an unsatisfactory drama called *Insult*, a film version of *The Good Companions* (in which he couldn't really compete with the screen looks and charm of Jessie Matthews) and a frustrating (at least from Gielgud's point of view) Hitchcock thriller, *The Secret Agent*. The films brought him useful money and exposure outside London, but his heart – and his soul – were still totally committed to the theatre.

His next stage success was a considerable one. Under the name Gordon Daviot, Elizabeth Mackintosh (who also wrote as Josephine Tey) had written a play called *Richard of Bordeaux*. She had been inspired by Gielgud's portrayal of Richard II at the Vic, but hers was a simpler, sweeter, more popular version of the story. John had reservations about the piece when he first read it, but having tried it out at the Arts Theatre and having worked on the script and revised it with Gordon Daviot, he opened in it at the New Theatre in February 1932. It was an immediate and spectacular triumph. *The Daily Telegraph*'s critic, W. A. Darlington, reported that the audience gave it 'a glorious and full-throated roar such as the West End seldom hears in these sophisticated days.'

Gielgud directed the play himself, with stunning costumes and sets created by 'Motley', a team of three designers – Margaret and Sophie Harris and Elizabeth Montgomery – who were to work regularly and very happily with John over the next decade. The company included his first Juliet, Gwen Ffrangcon-Davies (said Agate, if she 'is not the best actress in England there is certainly none better'), his old friend George Howe and the not over-friendly Donald Wolfit, but the star of the evening was Gielgud: 'a superb performance', 'masterly', 'effortless', 'serene'. He was at the summit – and loving it.

Emlyn Williams called on him during the run of *Richard of Bordeaux*. 'I must remember to order three hundred more postcards,' said John. 'After the show I sit signing them in my costume as people come round. Yes, I know it's vulgar but I can't resist it. I'm a star!'

'The world's best Hamlet'

Early in the summer of 1934 a friend said to Emlyn Williams, 'John's doing *The Maitlands*, the new Mackenzie piece. . . . It's modern, of course. John says if his public don't see him soon in a pair of trousers they'll think he hasn't got any.'

After *Richard of Bordeaux* Gielgud was anxious to appear in 'something entirely different'. For many *The Maitlands*, in which he played a dowdy schoolmaster, was altogether too different. It was Ronald Mackenzie's last play, completed shortly before he was killed in a car crash, and Komis, who directed it, persuaded John to take on the less glamorous of the two leading parts in a deliberate attempt to get him to play against what his public might conceive as the Gielgud persona. Some of the public were disappointed – and a few expressed their disapproval from the gallery on the first night – but on the whole the critics were generous and Ivor Brown found in Gielgud's performance 'all his poignant quality' plus 'a new masculinity of attack to suit the energy of the writing'.

Previous page: Hamlet, *New Theatre, 1934.*

Below: with Sophie Stewart in The Maitlands, *Wyndham's, 1934.*

SEPTEMBER, 1934

The PLAY of the MOMENT

117

"THE MAITLANDS"

SOPHIE STEWART and JOHN GIELGUD in "The Maitlands," presented by Howard Wyndham and Bronson Albery, at Wyndham's Theatre from the late Ronald Mackenzie's deeply interesting play,

Since the end of the run of *The Good Companions* in 1931 Gielgud had been under contract to Bronson Albery, the impresario and manager of the Criterion, Wyndham's and New theatres. His first venture with Albery had been in another, generally better regarded, Mackenzie play, *Musical Chairs*, but now, towards the end of *The Maitlands'* four month run, Albery suggested to Gielgud that he should appear in and direct a new production of *Hamlet* to open at the New in November 1934. The invitation to return to the part with which he had had such a success at the Vic – but this time with longer for rehearsal, a more generous budget, and designs by the beloved Motleys – was irresistible. Gielgud cast the twenty-five-year-old Jessica Tandy as Ophelia, with Laura Cowie as Gertrude, Frank Vosper as Claudius, George Howe as Polonius, Glen Byam Shaw as Laertes, Jack Hawkins as Horatio

Hamlet

'To play the part of Hamlet is the ambition of every young actor . . . The part demands declamation, macabre humour, passionate violence, philosophical reflection . . . Hamlet is the many-sided, many-talented Elizabethan man – prince, son, courtier, swordsman, philosopher, lover, friend.' Gielgud played the part first at the Old Vic in 1930.

Hamlet at the New Theatre

*Top : Hamlet (**John Gielgud**).*
    *Ophelia (**Jessica Tandy**).*

*Bottom : Claudius (**Frank Vosper**).*
    Hamlet.

Centre : Hamlet and Gertrude
    *(**Laura Cowie**).*

Bottom : Ophelia and Laertes
    *(**Glen Byam Shaw**).*

*Top : Polonius (**George Howe**).*
    Ophelia.

*Bottom : Horatio (**Jack Hawkins**).*
    Hamlet.

Opposite: Hamlet, *New Theatre,*
1934.

Below: *with Judith Anderson as*
Gertrude, the North American tour,
1936.

Opposite: Hamlet *in 1939.*

*Below: with Fay Compton as Ophelia,
Elsinore, 1939.*

Hamlet, *Haymarket, 1944, below and opposite.*

and Alec Guinness as Osric. J. C. Trewin called the production 'the key Shakespearean revival of its period', but it was not a total critical triumph. Raymond Mortimer considered John's Hamlet 'too purely the intellectual', and Agate reckoned it was 'Everest half scaled'. But whatever the critics thought, the public was unequivocally enthusiastic and the production ran for 132 performances, a record beaten previously only by Henry Irving and subsequently only by Richard Burton in Gielgud's own production in New York in 1964.

Now that John was back in period clothes that's how he was to stay for his next ten stage appearances. The first of these was the title part in André Obey's *Noah*, adapted into English by John and his director Michel Saint-Denis who had been responsible for the original Compagnie des Quinze production in 1931. The

NEW THEATRE
ST. MARTIN'S LANE, W.C.2

Licensed by the Lord Chamberlain to HOWARD WYNDHAM

Photo by Howard Coster

JOHN GIELGUD
as NOAH

2g July 1935

Lessees
THE WYNDHAM THEATRES, Ltd.

Managing Directors
HOWARD WYNDHAM and BRONSON ALBERY

'A mixture of Lear, Job, Tolstoy and the Old Man of the Sea. . .' John Gielgud as Noah at the New Theatre, 1935.

Noah (Mr. JOHN GIELGUD). "WHAT A RELIEF TO GET AWAY FROM THOSE WILD PEOPLE FOR A TIME!"

make-up and costume made Gielgud virtually unrecognizable. Ivor Brown described his Noah as a 'mixture of Lear, Job, Tolstoy and the Old Man of the Sea plagued with a Load of Mischief'. In general the public was both charmed and intrigued by the piece and by John's performance. The reaction from *Punch* was typical: 'It has recently been made plain that descendants are entitled to object to plays about their ancestors, and it is thought quite natural, in an age of realism on the stage, that they should object furiously to the bare idea. But none of the descendents of Noah who watched Mr John Gielgud take him out of the family frame and make him walk and talk at the New Theatre, would have dreamt of invoking privilege to stop him. For Noah is a credit to us all. Of the type of Daniel Peggotty, with moments of Mr Micawber, he is, in Mr Gielgud's hands, something much more than a delightful old boy. He is man the builder and maker – but even more, man the servant of God.'

In the autumn of 1935 John had hoped to star in a stage version of Dickens' *A Tale of Two Cities* on which he had been working with the young Terence Rattigan, but the project had to be abandoned when Sir John Martin Harvey, who was now seventy-two and had been playing in his own adaptation of the same novel since 1899, announced that he was contemplating making another farewell tour with his own production and complained that the Gielgud enterprise would present unfair competition. Out of deference to the old actor-manager, Gielgud reluctantly shelved his own plan and proposed an alternative, and equally ambitious, venture, to Bronson Albery: a new production of *Romeo and Juliet* with Peggy Ashcroft as Juliet, Edith Evans as the Nurse, and with Gielgud himself both directing and alternating the roles of Romeo and Mercutio with Robert Donat.

Albery bought the idea immediately, but Donat declined the invitation. In his place Gielgud cast a twenty-eight-year-old rising star, Laurence Olivier. They had worked together only once before, in John's production of Gordon Daviot's *Queen of Scots* the year before, in which at the last minute Olivier had played Bothwell when Ralph Richardson withdrew from the part. When *Romeo and Juliet* opened at the New Theatre in October 1935 Olivier played Romeo and Gielgud Mercutio. At the end of November they swopped roles and Gielgud stayed as Romeo for the duration of the run which continued until the end of March, making it the longest run of the play on record.

Those who saw both players in both roles tended to endorse Herbert Farjeon's verdict: 'As Romeo Mr Olivier was about twenty times as much in love with Juliet as Mr Gielgud is. But Mr Gielgud speaks most of the poetry far better than Mr Olivier. ... Yet – I must out with it – the fire of Mr Olivier's passion carried the play along as Mr Gielgud's doesn't quite.' Looking back on the production fifteen years later, another critic, J. C. Trewin, clearly felt the same way: 'It was fashionable in those days to hold that Olivier could not speak the verse: he was blamed for his staccato delivery and dry tone. Even so, I thought perversely that his Romeo caressed certain of the lines as no other player in my recol-

Romeo and Juliet

At the New Theatre, 1935: Gielgud as Romeo, with Peggy Ashcroft as Juliet.

lection – not even Gielgud – had done. ... The actor looked superb: half the battle was won when his Romeo walked upon the New Theatre stage straight from that Verona of hot sun, sharp swords, brief lives, and the nightingale beneath the moon ... Olivier was a hearty, swaggering Mercutio; but Romeo is first; it is still his voice that I set to many of the lines in the part, just as Gielgud's voice will always speak my Hamlet and Cassius.'

In rehearsals Gielgud was highly critical of Olivier's delivery but in performance he was aware that the younger actor was able to achieve a reality in the part that eluded him. 'I bullied him a great deal about his verse-speaking, which, he admitted himself, he wasn't happy about. I was rather showy about mine, and fancied myself very much as a verse speaker, and I became very mannered in consequence. But I was so jealous, because not only did he play Romeo with tremendous energy but he knew just how to cope with it and select. I remember Ralph Richardson saying to me, "But you see, when Larry leans against the balcony and looks up, then you have the whole scene, immediately". ... I had been draping myself around the stage for weeks, thinking myself very romantic as Romeo, and I was rather baffled and dismayed to find that I couldn't achieve the same effect at all.'

omeo and Juliet, *New Theatre,*
935: opposite, top: Laurence Olivier
s Romeo, Edith Evans as the Nurse
nd John Gielgud as Mercutio and
elow: Gielgud as Romeo, Olivier as
Mercutio.

Peggy Ashcroft, who of course was Juliet to them both, echoed Richardson. 'I thought John's extraordinary, darting imagination made him the better Mercutio, but Larry was the definitive Romeo, a real, vigorous, impulsive youth.'

Peggy Ashcroft and Edith Evans stayed with Gielgud for his next production for Albery at the New Theatre. As *Punch* reported, it was the first full-scale West End production of a Chekhov play. The author 'would surely feel elated could he see with what honour the English stage is handling *The Seagull* now at the New Theatre. A cluster of stars, fully supported, are directed by Komisarjevsky and act in costumes and scenes which omit no detail, that can throw an almost fierce light on the texture of the play. That is the peril of very good acting, that it will show up in the sunlight defects of the dramatist that a less complete mastery of the characters and situations might have left in a kindly blur.

'But *The Seagull* is full of meat; there are in Chekhov no minor characters: to come on the stage at all is to be a human soul, aspiring and suffering and poignant.'

Punch was clearly impressed with Komisarjevsky's achievement: 'The mood and the time are brilliantly recaptured and displayed in a masterly production which holds the attention with increasing intensity through four acts and three hours.'

Gielgud too admired Komis's overall handling of the play – 'sensational, it really was a most beautiful production' – though at the time he (and several of the critics) had reservations about the way the director had insisted that John play Trigorin as a dandified gigolo rather than the down-at-heel figure Chekhov himself was known to have envisaged.

The Seagull was a success, but Gielgud was only able to stay in it for six weeks as he was readying himself for his next venture: a new production of *Hamlet*, to be presented on Broadway and directed by Guthrie McClintic, with Lillian Gish as Ophelia, Judith Anderson as Gertrude and an almost all-American cast. The production opened at the Alexandra Theater, Toronto, in September and came to the St James's Theater in New York in October. The Broadway first night audience was ecstatic; the press was generous, but rather more reserved. The production received an unusual boost from an unexpected quarter when, only a month after it had opened, a rival *Hamlet* starring Leslie Howard also arrived on Broadway. Of the two, John's was undoubtedly the better received and the fortuitous competition between the productions seemed to fuel the public's interest in the play and increase their enthusiasm for the Gielgud interpretation.

At the end of the New York run in January 1937, the production went on a brief tour, taking in Boston, Philadelphia and Washington D.C. where John and Lillian Gish were invited to the White House, introduced to the President (who was 'charming, urbane and gracious' according to Gielgud) and given tea by Mrs Roosevelt. By the time he had completed his American run of *Hamlet* Gielgud had given more than four hundred performances of the role, but he wasn't finished with it yet.

In 1939 he was invited to give his *Hamlet* in Denmark at the

OMEO WHO TOOK THE ORCHARD WALL IN
YLE, BUT FAILED AT THE BALCONY-JUMP.

iet . . . . . Miss Peggy Ashcroft
neo . . . . . Mr. Laurence Olivier.

Gielgud as Mercutio: 'My scheme of alternating the parts of Romeo and Mercutio with Olivier had proved very attractive to the public, and showed that it was possible to play two great parts in completely different ways without upsetting the swing and rhythm of the whole production. The only trouble came in our scenes together, when we kept on trying to speak on each other's cues.'

Castle at Elsinore. This time Fay Compton played Ophelia, with Laura Cowie as Gertrude, Jack Hawkins doubling as Claudius and the Ghost, George Howe by now an almost definitive Polonius, Glen Byam Shaw as Horatio, Harry Andrews as Laertes and Marius Goring as the First Player. Before setting off for Denmark, John gave six performances of the play at Sir Henry Irving's old theatre, the Lyceum in Wellington Street. It was the last production staged there before the building was converted into a dance hall. At Elsinore, as in London, the new *Hamlet* was warmly received. The journalist George W. Bishop was there: 'On a calm evening in July, 1939, following a somewhat stormy afternoon, John Gielgud acted Hamlet at Elsinore. I was present when he was greeted on arrival by a salute from two small cannon on the battlements and on the morning following his first performance in the courtyard of Kronborg by the greatest praise in print that probably even he has ever received. The Copenhagen papers were headlined: "The World's Best Hamlet" and the *Berlingske Tidende* described the event as "the biggest occasion in the theatre for years". The dramatic critic of *Politiken* said: "The evening was Gielgud's. Never has English sounded more beautiful from the human mouth."'

Gielgud returned to *Hamlet* yet again in 1944, this time with Peggy Ashcroft as Ophelia. Feeling the need for a fresh approach, he didn't direct it himself, but asked the Cambridge don George Rylands, celebrated for his undergraduate productions of Shakespeare, to take on the play. This proved a mistake: the company resented Rylands' didactic approach, and, although many considered this to be John's most successful Hamlet, he wasn't happy about it. He was now forty and conscious of his age. 'I was well aware that, with the help of various directors and actors with whom I'd worked over fifteen years, I knew more about the part, had better staying power, and perhaps more selectivity. But I didn't think I could contrive the opening of the play in the way that it had come to me when I was absolutely fresh, because I really felt it then; I was young and so I naturally put it over in the right way. But later I tried to imitate that, and I felt false.'

He took on the role one last time in 1945, once more in a production of his own as part of an ENSA tour in the Middle and Far East. He played the part for the very last time at the Cairo Opera House in February 1946. Among the young servicemen who saw Gielgud's ENSA *Hamlet* more than once was Donald Sinden. His admiration was absolute: 'The untold depths of misery he could dredge up in any of Hamlet's lines: the gravity he gave to "A little more than kin, and less than kind". After Hamlet had seen and talked with his father's ghost he says to himself:

> The time is out of joint: O cursed spite,
> That ever I was born to set it right!

then he turns to Horatio and Marcellus and says, "Nay, come, let's go together". I wish I could describe how many facets Gielgud gave to that simple line. ('Please go with me.' 'I don't want to let you out of my sight.' 'It would look better if we arrived

together.' 'Let us leave this awesome place.' 'Don't leave me.')
I learned from that one line what infinite possibilities are open
to an actor.'

Gielgud himself may not have been convinced by the Hamlet
he portrayed once he had turned forty, but others had no such
reservations. According to Sybil Thorndike, 'Those who saw the
Hamlet of John Gielgud have a memory of something hauntingly
beautiful for which to be grateful all their lives.' And James Agate
had no doubt that the 1944 Hamlet was Gielgud's finest: 'Mr
Gielgud is now completely and authoritatively master of this
tremendous part. He is, we feel, this generation's rightful tenant
of this "monstrous Gothic castle of a poem". He has acquired an
almost Irvingesque quality of pathos, and in the passages after
the play scene an incisiveness, a raillery, a mordancy worthy of
the Old Man. He imposes on us this play's questing feverishness.
The middle act gives us ninety minutes of high excitement and
assured virtuosity; Forbes-Robertson was not more bedazzling in
the "O, what a rogue and peasant slave" soliloquy. In short, I
hold that this is, and is likely to remain, the best Hamlet of our
time.'

'The finest flower of
the contemporary stage'

For the complete man of the theatre – as Gielgud certainly was by the mid-1930s – his first forays into management were surprisingly unlucky. In 1933 Emlyn Williams had sent him his play *Spring 1600*. John liked it and wanted to direct it. When Bronson Albery said he didn't want to produce, Gielgud decided to turn impresario and, together with his friend Richard Clowes (whose father nobly offered to help secure the financial backing), presented the play at the Shaftesbury in January 1934. It was an elaborate production – with ambitious settings designed by Motley, a large number of walk-ons in addition to the not uncostly cast, a chorus of singers and a substantial orchestra – and in the event proved to be an expensive flop. The notices were fair, but the customers didn't come and the show closed in a few weeks.

A year later Rodney Ackland brought John his adaptation of Hugh Walpole's *The Old Ladies*. Again John liked it, wanted to direct it and when Albery declined to become involved, teamed up once more with Richard Clowes (and his munificent father) and presented it himself, first at the New Theatre, then at the smaller St Martin's. The production was less expensive and the notices creditable ('Not for months have I heard any audience cheer as last night's did' – W. A. Darlington), but business was poor and again the play only survived a matter of weeks.

In the Spring of 1937, immediately after the American tour of *Hamlet*, Gielgud produced a second play by Emlyn Williams, this time in partnership with the author. Emlyn had written *He Was Born Gay* for John and since the subject was the life in England of Louis XV's lost son, 'a romantic half-mad princeling' and Gielgud was ready to star in the piece as well as co-present and co-direct it, from the commercial viewpoint the project looked more promising than either of its predecessors. In fact, it was the least successful of the three. After a short pre-London tour the play opened at the Queen's in May only to close within a fortnight, after just twelve performances.

Having failed conspicuously with three new plays, for Gielgud's next managerial enterprise he turned back to the classics, to dead authors whose worth and work and popularity with the public he could more readily rely on. In the early summer of 1937 he decided the time was right to attempt to realise an ambition he had been nurturing for several years: to form his own permanent company and present a full season of plays in London under his own management. At the end of the season, Michel Saint-Denis, who was involved in the venture, described its genesis: 'The idea of forming a permanent company did not occur to Gielgud suddenly. He was already talking about it when I produced *Noah* with him. It took shape slowly during the four years of his work at the New Theatre and culminated with the success of *The Seagull*, produced by Komisarjevsky. The nucleus of the company was, in fact, formed at that time. He surrounded himself with first-class actors and a group of very capable and enthusiastic young actors. He did not try to show himself as a solo actor. He cared more about the ensemble. He invited Tyrone Guthrie and Komis-

Previous page: as John Worthing in The Importance of Being Earnest, *Globe, 1939.*

Opposite and below: John Gielgud's Season at the Queen's Theatre in 1937 opened with Richard II, *followed by* The School for Scandal, *caricatured by Tom Titt in the* Tatler.

Dress Rehearsal. Sat. Sept. 4. 1937

QUEEN'S THEATRE

JOHN GIELGUD'S SEASON

6ᵈ·

RICHARD II

by

WILLIAM SHAKESPEARE

PROGRAMME

arjevsky to produce for him. Then, because Komisarjevsky was not free, I was asked. He chose four strong classical plays of different styles for his repertory. The public would be able to watch the same actors in their interpretation of great characters of various periods. The plays were put on for eight weeks minimum and ten weeks maximum. Each producer was offered the possibility of seven or nine weeks' rehearsals. Security was given to the actors for a period of nine months. The leading members of the cast worked on a percentage basis, and so did the guest-actors who were specially engaged for one or more plays during the course of the season. Thus it was made possible for a large number of leading actors to work together.'

Living as we do now in the age of subsidised national companies where an eight-week rehearsal period for a play is considered commonplace, it is difficult to appreciate how revolutionary Gielgud's enterprise was. At the Old Vic the company might remain the same for a season, but the plays were rehearsed in three weeks. In the commercial theatre, a cast was brought together for each individual play, rehearsed for three weeks and perhaps given a brief pre-London tour before embarking on an as-long-as-possible West End run. There were other actor-managers who produced a repertoire of plays with the same company, but usually with the notion of presenting themselves as the star attraction and not with the ideal of creating an 'ensemble' in mind. In retrospect it is easy to take Gielgud's 1937/38 season at the Queen's almost for granted, to dismiss it as simply a successful quartet of plays with all-star casts and so fail to recognise it for the pioneering achievement it was. At the time – several years before the Olivier/ Richardson Old Vic seasons at the New after the war and many years before the creation of the Royal Shakespeare Company and the National Theatre – Saint-Denis was one of those who realised that what was achieved in 1937/38 would have 'important consequences'. He put it very simply: 'If good work was done it was because the conditions of work were so much better than in the average theatre.'

And good work certainly was done. The season opened and closed with Shakespeare, *Richard II* and *The Merchant of Venice*, with *The School for Scandal* and *The Three Sisters* in between. The plays were scheduled to run for eight to ten weeks preceded by up to nine weeks of rehearsals. Most of the actors had never known such a luxury, indeed regarded it as a self-indulgence, but all were convinced by the experience. Gwen Ffrangcon-Davies, who with Angela Baddeley and Carol Goodner was one of the guest stars engaged to appear in only one or two of the plays, was apprehensive before rehearsals began, but after seven weeks admitted, 'I have never had the opportunity of working for such a long time. I thought I would be stale, but on the contrary, it changes one's whole attitude to one's work.'

The company was a fine one, led by John himself, who appeared in all four plays, with Peggy Ashcroft, other old friends like George Howe, Leon Quatermaine, Harcourt Williams, plus younger players like George Devine, Harry Andrews, Alec Guinness and Michael Redgrave. Gielgud launched the season with *Richard II*, directing as well as playing the title role, because it was a part he knew well and could approach with confidence. 'John, even at the first reading, was as near perfect as I could wish or imagine,' Michael Redgrave recalled. 'Ninety per cent of the beauty of his acting was the beauty of his voice. To this day I can see no way of improving on the dazzling virtuosity of phrasing and breathing which was Gielgud's in the cadenza beginning:

> Draw near,
> And list what with our council we have done . . .'

Some critics found fault with Motley's over-decorated settings (and a few of John's friends found fault with his over-decorated performance: 'Act on the lines, not in between them' said Granville-Barker), but overall the production was acclaimed. The eulogy in the *Illustrated Sporting and Dramatic News* was not untypical: 'The season which John Gielgud has begun so auspiciously by presenting, producing and playing *Richard II*, bids fair to be the most important that the English Theatre has known

Opposite: Richard II in his own production, 1937.

Joseph Surface in Tyrone Guthrie's production of The School for Scandal, *1937.*

for some years. Unlike the actor-managers of tradition, Mr Gielgud chooses to surround himself with the finest flower of the contemporary stage; and advisedly, for he can pit his genius against the greatest odds. The greatest odds, on this occasion took the form of Leon Quartermaine who, as John of Gaunt, gave a towering performance which already had become a legend by the time the curtain fell.'

The School for Scandal was given a cooler reception. Gielgud presented a deliberately unsympathetic Joseph Surface, which some of his loyal followers found uncomfortable, though Olivier regarded it as 'the best light comedy performance I've ever seen or ever shall'. The production, too, directed by Tyrone Guthrie, came in for criticism: some saw it as too busy and contrived, others as too earthy and mundane. Michel Saint-Denis's version of *The Three Sisters*, on the other hand, was universally hailed as a masterpiece. Herbert Farjeon spoke for all: 'It is in the order of things that a critic should praise this play. It is in the order of things that an audience, to signify appreciation, should applaud it. Yet one praises and one applauds with reluctance. Silence is

Vershinin in Michel Saint-Denis' production of The Three Sisters, *1938.*

the perfectest herald of joy. One is so overwhelmed by the poignant beauty of the production that anything written or spoken must fall far short of what one feels. Moreover, the emotional reaction is so personal, so private, that one is in no mood for eloquence . . . If Mr Gielgud's season at the Queen's had produced only this, it would have more than justified itself. There is a tenderness in the acting so exquisite that it is like the passing of light . . . Here, in short, is a production of the very first order of one of the masterpieces of dramatic literature.'

Gielgud admired the production ('Remarkable. Really stunning. Everybody said it was the best Chekhovian production that has ever been done in this country') though he didn't consider his own performance as Colonel Vershinin totally satisfactory. Nor was he very happy with his own Shylock, played not in the heroic Irving tradition, but as a shuffling, morose, malignant outsider. The public might have preferred something on a grander, less vulnerable, less credible scale, but many of Gielgud's colleagues – Olivier among them – regarded it as one of his finest characterisations.

Shylock in his production of The Merchant of Venice, *co-directed with Glen Byam Shaw, 1938.*

Of course, by the time he came to play Shylock and co-direct it with Glen Byam Shaw, Gielgud was weary. Though satisfying and gratifying – and even profitable – it had been a long, heavy season and when it came to an end and the company disbanded, John was happy to slough off his managerial yoke for a while and accept a handsome offer to star with Dame Marie Tempest in Dodie Smith's family comedy *Dear Octopus*, again directed by Byam Shaw. The invitation came from Hugh 'Binkie' Beaumont, whom John had first met more than a decade before when Binkie had been the business manager at Barnes and John had appeared in the Russian season there. Binkie was now the newly appointed managing director of H. M. Tennent and destined to be London's most influential and respected commercial management for a quarter of a century, during which time he remained one of John's closest friends and professional advisers, as well as being his most frequent employer.

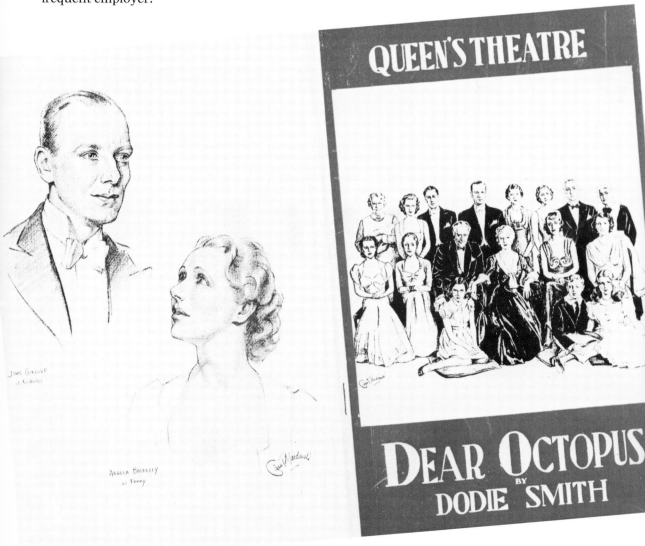

JOHN GIELGUD
as Nicholas

ANGELA BADDELEY
as Fenny

QUEEN'S THEATRE

DEAR OCTOPUS
BY
DODIE SMITH

Dear Octopus may have been a slight, sentimental comedy – and John may not have cared for his character ('rather dull, conventional, juvenile') – but it was also a considerable commercial success and Gielgud stayed in the play for eleven months, from August 1938 to June 1939. It was a time when the war clouds were gathering menacingly over Europe, but for John the affairs of nations always came a poor second to the world of the theatre which was and would always be his universe. It was during these uneasy days before the outbreak of war that he went to stay with Beverley Nichols. 'He arrived on an evening of acute international tension,' according to Nichols. 'We were sitting round in a state of unaccustomed gloom, wondering what was going to happen to us all, whether we should be able to finish our books or our poems or our paintings or our music, or whether we were all going to be swept up in the approaching holocaust. "If you're all so worried about what's going to happen," said John, "why don't you turn on the radio?" "There isn't one," I said. "That," replied John, "is excellent news, because I shall be able to listen to myself talking . . ." And talk he did, brilliantly, till the small hours of the morning – not about Hitler or Mussolini or any of the other ogres who were haunting us, but about the theatre, which was all he knew about or thought important in this distracted world.

'On the following morning I rose early, to get the papers from the village post office. But I found that John had forestalled me. He was sitting in the music room, surrounded by scattered copies of the Sunday papers, whose headlines were double-decked with disaster. Ultimatums, troop movements, diplomatic scurryings, mobilisations. His face was dark.

'"What in heaven's name has happened?" I demanded.

'His face grew darker. But he had not noticed the headlines. He was scanning the theatrical pages.

'"The worst," he proclaimed in sepulchral tones. "Gladys has got the most appalling notices. And so has the play." He strode to the window and stared out. "I don't know what the world is coming to."'

Before embarking on the rehearsals for *Dear Octopus*, Gielgud had directed *Spring Meeting*, a play with an Irish setting, starring Margaret Rutherford. It was written by John Perry (a close friend and colleague of John's and Binkie's) and Molly Skrine (better known then as M. J. Farrell and now as Molly Keane) and ran for a year at the Ambassadors. Over the next decade Gielgud directed another eight plays in which he didn't appear himself, the most notable of which was probably *The Beggar's Opera* at the Haymarket in the Spring of 1940, with Michael Redgrave leading a Glyndebourne company. When Redgrave was ill, John went on and sang Macheath himself for four performances. Nobody asked for their money back.

After *Hamlet* at the Lyceum and at Elsinore, Gielgud returned to John Worthing in *The Importance of Being Earnest*. With Joyce Carey and Angela Baddeley as Gwendolyn and Cecily, Ronald Ward as Algernon and Edith Evans as the definitive Lady Bracknell, the production at the Globe was a resounding success, despite

the fact that war was declared early in the run – or, perhaps, in part, because of it. Gielgud revived the production in 1941, again at the Globe and again with Edith Evans, but with Jack Hawkins as Algernon and Gwen Ffrangcon-Davies and Peggy Ashcroft as the girls. Of the earlier production *The Times* declared, 'If the past theatrical decade had to be represented by a single production, this is the one that many good judges would choose.' And Tyrone Guthrie, not a man readily given to hyperbole, spoke of the 1941 production establishing the high water mark of artificial comedy 'in our era'.

A year later, at the Phoenix, he revived the play again, with the same trio of leading ladies, but with Cyril Ritchard in place of Jack Hawkins and Jean Cadell replacing Margaret Rutherford as Miss Prism. His final revival was one he took to Canada and the United States in 1947, this time with Margaret Rutherford as a much less imperious Lady Bracknell, Robert Flemyng as Algy and Pamela Brown and Jane Baxter as the girls. When it opened at the Royale in New York, the play was as warmly welcomed as the earlier English revivals had been, though Gielgud himself realised that it was a piece that didn't benefit from long runs: 'When we played it too long and lost the inner feeling of fun, it wasn't funny any more. This was interesting, because it has to be played with the most enormous solemnity. But inside you must play the whole play as if you were doing a practical joke

Hamlet, 1 July, 1939 – the final curtain call on the last night of the Lyceum Theatre; Gielgud with, left to right, Jack Hawkins, George Howe, Fay Compton and Laura Cowie.

Opposite: The Importance of Being Earnest, *The Globe, 1939; the programme has become a collector's item because of the delicious misprint.*

Globe Theatre

The Importance of Being Ernest

ANGUS McBEAN

The Importance of Being Earnest

'The more elegantly the actors give and take, the more will the intrinsic quality of the wit emerge, as the grave puppet characters utter their delicate cadences and spin their web of preposterously elegant sophistication.'

Opposite: With Gwen Ffrangcon-Davies as Gwendolen and Edith Evans as Lady Bracknell at the Globe, 1940. Above: With Gwen Ffrangcon-Davies at the Phoenix, 1942. Right: With Margaret Rutherford as Lady Bracknell at the Royale, New York, 1947.

–with immense seriousness, knowing yourself that you are being killingly funny. And yet if you were to betray with the slightest flicker of an eyelash that you know you're funny, you are not funny either. When we lost the inner fun after six or eight months – when we got sick of the play – it immediately told and the play became a sort of affected exercise.'

In the spring of 1940, with the first revival of *The Importance* and the Redgrave *Beggar's Opera* now behind him, Gielgud returned to the Old Vic for the first time in almost a decade. With Tyrone Guthrie and Lewis Casson as his collaborators, John presented a short season of Shakespeare – *King Lear* and *The Tempest* – with a distinguished company including Jessica Tandy, Fay Compton, Cathleen Nesbitt, Robert Harris, Jack Hawkins and Marius Goring. Harley Granville-Barker was invited over from his home in Paris to direct *Lear*. He declined to take full command

Old Vic, 1940. 'Lear is in your grasp': Angus McBean's photograph shows Gielgud as Lear with Stephen Haggard as the Fool. Ronson's caricature includes Lewis Casson who played Kent as well as co-directing the production with Harley Granville-Barker.

or to have his name on the billing, but agreed to come and work with the company for about ten days. For John, 'they were the fullest in experience that I have ever had in all my years upon the stage.' Looking back on that time twenty-five years later, Gielgud described Granville-Barker's working methods: 'He used to come every day to the Vic and rehearse, looking like a marvellous surgeon. The company was transported. I never saw actors watch a director with such utter admiration and obedience. It was like Toscanini coming to rehearsal – very quiet, business suit, red eyebrows, and text in his hand. And I was so angry because there was nobody there to take his overcoat, or take notes for him, and he filled every moment; so much so that people didn't even go to try on their wigs, or have a bun, or anything – they just sat there. I got actors and actresses, from outside, friends of mine, to come and peek in, because I said "You really must see

The Tempest. *Gielgud as Prospero, with Marius Goring, who played Ariel as well as co-directing the production with George Devine.*

these rehearsals, they're something absolutely extraordinary." And we would go on until quite late at night. I remember doing the death scene of Lear with him, and he began stopping me on every word, and I thought every moment he'd say, "Now stop, don't act any more, we'll just work it out for technical effects." Not at all, he didn't say stop, so I went on acting and crying and carrying on, and trying to take the corrections as he gave them to me. And when I looked at my watch, we had been working on this short scene for forty minutes. But it was extraordinary that he had the skill not to make you wild and not to exhaust you so much that you couldn't go on; if you had the strength to go along with him, he could give you more than any person I ever met in my life.'

When they began work on the play together Granville-Barker had told John, 'Lear should be an oak, you're an ash; now we've got to do something about that.' The play was generally well received, though not all the critics felt that Gielgud's Lear was sufficiently the oak. Granville-Barker himself was well satisfied with his pupil's achievement. On 14 April he wrote to him:

> The Athenaeum,
> Pall Mall, S.W.1
> Sunday morning
>
> My dear Gielgud. Lear is in your grasp.
> Forget all the things I have bothered you about. Let your own now well self-disciplined instincts carry you along, and up; simply allowing the checks and changes to prevent your being carried *away*. And I prophesy – happily – great things for you.
>
> Yrs,
> H.G.B.

The fall of France coincided with the Old Vic season and Gielgud was conscious of the fact that what he called 'the smell of the times' both infected the play and enhanced the audience's receptivity to it: 'People used to come around and say, "This play is absolutely extraordinary, it's given us such pride," and I'd say, "But how can you bear it – this tearing out of the eyes, the death of the king, the cruelty . . ." But they would say, "Well, there's a kind of catharsis, and when we come out of the theatre we are uplifted, like after hearing Beethoven. It shows that with all the appalling horror that is going on – there is some glory, and something that's worth everything." This seemed to me extraordinary, and I felt it so deeply; we all did in the company at that time,'

Lear was followed by Prospero and John's 'scholarly Italian nobleman' in the production directed by George Devine and Marius Goring (and without assistance from Granville-Barker) and was well regarded. Symbolically enough, *The Tempest* was to be the Old Vic's last play for a decade. At the end of the run on 22 June 1940, the theatre closed its doors. Eleven months later it was severely damaged by enemy bombing.

Gielgud's own contribution to the war effort now took the form of a series of lectures devised by Ivor Brown entitled *Shakespeare – in Peace and War* (a talk-cum-recital that culminated inevitably with the show-stopping 'Once more unto the breach' speech from *Henry V*) followed by a tour of military bases with a programme of three short pieces: *Fumed Oak* and *Hands Across the Sea*, two of the one-act plays from Coward's *Tonight at 8.30* and *Hard Luck Story*, Gielgud's own adaptation of Chekhov's playlet *Swan Song* about an old actor rehearsing in a deserted theatre with only an ancient prompter for an audience.

In 1940 he made another film, *The Prime Minister*, an indifferent historical pageant about Disraeli in which John neither imitated nor rivalled George Arliss's definitive screen portrayal. Immediately the film was completed Gielgud returned to the war-ravaged West End where many of the theatres that had chosen to close at the onset of war and then been forced to close during the worst of the blitz, were now doing their best to maintain a policy of 'business as usual'. The vehicle Gielgud chose for himself was J. M. Barrie's gentle fantasy *Dear Brutus*, which had enjoyed its first success during the Great War. As theatre it may be fairly

Dear Brutus, *The Globe, 1941. 'I saw* Dear Brutus *on its first night in 1917 and afterwards in several revivals. When I directed and acted in it myself during the Second War, I kept remembering how marvellous Du Maurier had been as the painter Dearth. I could not touch him in the part.'*

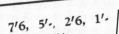

GLOBE THEATRE
SHAFTESBURY AVENUE, W.1.
Kindly loaned by Globe and Queen's Theatres Ltd.

THREE LECTURES
on
TUESDAY, JANUARY 30th
TUESDAY, FEBRUARY 6th
SUNDAY, FEBRUARY 11th
at 2-30

MR.

JOHN GIELGUD
on

"Shakespeare—
in Peace and War"
By IVOR BROWN

with

Excerpts from the Plays

IN AID OF
THE POLISH RELIEF FUND

ADMISSION - 7'6, 5'-, 2'6, 1'-
BOOK YOUR SEATS NOW!

Obtainable from Mrs. Edome Johnson, Appeals Secretary, Polish Relief
10, Grosvenor Place, S.W.1., or Theatre Box Office ('Phone: Gerrard

John Waddington Ltd., London: and Leeds

War Work: from London's Globe Theatre to the Cairo Opera House, from Gilbraltar to Burma, in Shakespeare, Coward and Chekhov.

flimsy, 'no more than a whimsey' but the public took to it and it ran at the Globe from January to May, when John took it on tour, first commercially, then for ENSA.

In 1942 and 1943 Gielgud also returned to two of the roles he had first essayed in his twenties: Macbeth, and Valentine in *Love for Love*. He found this second Macbeth less satisfactory than his first in 1930. It was persuasive but not towering, again the timbre was wrong. Robert Speaight was not alone in applauding the 'imaginative intensity' and 'deep psychological insight', while feeling 'only the warrior's muscle was missing'. After seeing the

As Valentine in Congreve's Love for Love *at the Phoenix, at the Haymarket and on tour in 1943 and 1944.*

Opposite: 'In 1942 I played Macbeth
for nearly a whole year . . . It was
exhausting and not very successful, but
ran quite a long time considering it is
such a desperately difficult play and
traditionally so very unlucky.'

performance James Agate wrote in his journal: 'John will never
be happy vocally with Macbeth; his voice is neither deep enough
nor resonant enough. But what sheer acting ability can do, he
does. He is the only Macbeth I have ever seen who has kept it
up all the way through; the last act, where most of them fall down,
is superb.'

His second Valentine, by contrast, was an unmitigated success.
Among its numerous avid admirers was the precocious Kenneth
Tynan who saw it, aged seventeen, and reported: 'Tongue-in-
cheek and hand-on-heart, he played the mock-madness scenes
as a sort of burlesque of his own Hamlet: he extended the intense
raptness, the silent inner lightnings which he shares with Irving,
until they reached delicious absurdity, Gielgud is an actor who
refuses to compromise with his audience: he does not offer a
welcoming hand, but binds a spell instead.'

Gielgud played Valentine on tour in the Spring of 1943 and
then for a year's run in the West End, at the Phoenix and the
Haymarket. With *Hamlet* and Somerset Maugham's *The Circle* (in

*In The Circle, 1944, the cast also
included Rosalie Crutchley (seated left)
and Yvonne Arnaud (seated centre). 'I
have always thought I was rather good
in unsympathetic parts – in The
Circle, for instance, as the husband
who likes the antique furniture better
than his young wife.'*

which John was much acclaimed as and loved playing 'the furniture-conscious prim husband' Arnold Champion-Cheyney) he revived *Love for Love* in the Summer of 1944 for a further tour and a season at the Haymarket. The same season continued in early 1945 with *A Midsummer Night's Dream*, with Gielgud and Ashcroft as Oberon and Titania, in what was recognised as a heavy-handed production by the Oxford don Nevill Coghill, and *The Duchess of Malfi*, Webster's oppressive and, to John certainly, unsympathetic Jacobean tragedy, directed with little verve by Cambridge's answer to Nevill Coghill, George Rylands.

Opposite: 1945: with Marian Spencer in The Duchess of Malfi, *and below, with Peggy Ashcroft in* A Midsummer Night's Dream.

Opposite: As Raskolnikoff in Crime and Punishment *at the National Theater, New York, 1947. The American company included Lillian Gish and Dolly Haas.*

Gielgud's war culminated in the Autumn of 1945 with a long tour of the Middle and Far East, playing *Hamlet* for the fifth and final time and Charles Condomyne in Coward's *Blithe Spirit* for the first and last. At the end of the wearying tour – eighty shows in eighteen weeks plus his recital of *Shakespeare – In Peace and War* – Gielgud returned with plans to direct Robert Helpmann in Rodney Ackland's dramatisation of *Crime and Punishment*. In the event, Helpmann was taken ill so John agreed to play Raskolnikoff and Anthony Quayle took over as director. Edith Evans played Madame Marmaladoff and Peter Ustinov the Chief of Police. In his autobiography Ustinov paints a revealing picture of Gielgud at the time, touching on the curious mixture of shyness and vanity that are hallmarks of the man: 'John Gielgud is so contorted with shyness at first meetings that he makes a normally shy person like myself feel brash, and even boorish. And yet, despite this gossamer delicacy, there are the heights to rise to before an anonymous public, and an ego, totally invisible in the drawing-room, imperceptibly takes over. As the curtain fell on the first act of *Crime and Punishment* during the first performance, he suddenly trumpeted a message to us all. "If there are going to have to be all these people in the wings, they *must look at me!*" He found it impossible to play to backs turned in discretion, in order not to break his concentration. To hell with the concentration, once there were people he was hungry for faces!'

As Eustace Jackson in The Return of the Prodigal, *with Rachel Kempson, described by the* Evening Standard *as 'the best dressed and best acted bad play in London'.*

Crime and Punishment was tolerably received by most critics and enthusiastically by some. Agate declared that Gielgud's Raskolnikoff was 'the best thing after Hamlet he has ever given us.'

At the beginning of 1947 Gielgud set off for Canada and the United States and spent the next eighteen months there, playing in *The Importance*, *Love for Love*, *Crime and Punishment* (unsatisfactorily redirected by Komisarjevsky who rather despised the piece) and directing Judith Anderson and playing opposite her in a new version of Euripedes' *Medea*, in which she scored a personal success but he didn't. When he returned to England in the middle of 1948 – scotching rumours that he had abandoned the British theatre for good and was seeking American citizenship – he directed three plays in as many months, none of which enjoyed any great success, and then chose to make his West End comeback in St John Hankin's appropriately entitled but unhappily dated *The Return of the Prodigal*. It was not much of a success either.

Gielgud's fortunes were at a low ebb. He was still a great star, of course, never short of offers and lucrative ones at that, but he was aware that he had lost his sense of direction and whereas a few years before he had been the unchallenged leader of the profession, the reins had now slipped from his fingers. When Laurence Olivier played *Richard III* in the first of those glorious Old Vic seasons at the New Theatre in 1944, with characteristically impetuous generosity Gielgud had sent him the sword that Kean had used as Richard, the same sword that had been presented to Irving on his first night in the role, the sword that John's mother had passed on to him in his turn. Giving the sword to Olivier had in no sense been intended as a symbolic gesture, but John could not fail to recognise Olivier's ascendant star. When John returned to England, Olivier, three years his junior, had recently been knighted, had just completed his film of *Hamlet*, and was enjoying the kind of critical acclaim John had not known in ten years. For Gielgud, the most generous and giving of men, it was a perplexing and uncertain time. Peggy Ashcroft tells an endearing story about him. John was discussing Othello. 'I don't really know what jealousy is,' he said. Then he caught himself. 'Oh, yes, I do! I remember! When Larry had a success as Hamlet, I wept.'

'The true aristocrat of both tragedy and comedy'

'Gielgud has new chance of No. 1 place,' ran a headline in the London *Evening Standard* in the Spring of 1949. The article was prompted by the news that John was to star in Christopher Fry's latest play *The Lady's Not for Burning* and declared in no uncertain terms, 'Olivier is a first class actor and producer. But in my opinion Gielgud is the one genius of the contemporary English stage.'

Whether or not John's genius was put fully to the test in Fry's medieval verse comedy is debatable, but that Thomas Mendip provided him with his strongest role in a new play since *Richard of Bordeaux* and his first considerable success in several years was beyond dispute. The play was written for Alec Clunes who played it originally at the Arts Theatre, but when Clunes let his option on the play drop, Beaumont and Gielgud agreed it might make a marvellous vehicle for John. In rehearsal and on tour Gielgud had growing reservations about the play's chances of success and, with Fry, continued to work on the structure of the piece right up to the London first night – and even beyond. Gielgud's fears, however, proved unfounded. The play – with an evocative setting by Oliver Messel and a strong cast including Pamela Brown, Esmé Percy, Harcourt Williams, an eighteen-year-old Claire Bloom and a twenty-four-year-old Richard Burton – was an immediate success with critics and public alike, both in London in 1949 and again in New York two years later. Kenneth Tynan, now all of twenty-two, was one of those who enthused gently over the production, especially over Gielgud's handling of the verse: 'Gielgud, incomparably alert to Fry's poetry, demonstrated in *The Lady's Not For Burning* that here at least was dramatic verse which could be spoken at the speed of dramatic prose: not cryptic and solemn, needing sombre pointing and emphases, but trickling, skimming, darting like a salmon in a mountain stream. Mr Gielgud's company spoke better than any other group of players in England; and for this the credit must be his.'

1949 represented a turning-point in Gielgud's fortunes in another, perhaps even more significant way. Anthony Quayle had recently been appointed director of the Shakespeare Memorial Theatre at Stratford-upon-Avon and now he invited Gielgud to come to work at Stratford for the first time, to direct Diana Wynyard and Quayle himself as Beatrice and Benedick in *Much Ado About Nothing*. John leapt at the opportunity and with a fine company (the walk-ons, 'Watchmen, servants and dancers', included Jill Bennett, Margaret Courtenay, Michael Bates, Robert Hardy and Robert Shaw) gave the play a clear, dynamic and witty production that heralded his return to work of real substance, tackled with a lightness of touch and sureness of hand. For the 1950 season John revived and refined the production and played in it himself, with Peggy Ashcroft as his Beatrice. It was nothing short of a triumph. J. C. Trewin was there: 'Applause in a theatre, when it is earned, is to me as the spirit-stirring drum was to Othello. It is, I know, unfashionable in these days to show excitement. Rather, we should be ready to tilt the acid, light the fuse. Attack must come before appreciation. The theatre is a kind of

Previous page: John Gielgud as Joseph Surface in The School for Scandal, *1962.*

The Lady's Not for Burning, *with Eliot Makeham, Richard Leech and Harcourt Williams, the Globe, 1949.*

blood-sport, with the actors as Early Christians and ourselves as ravenous lions. Absurd! Nothing enlivens the theatre more than enthusiasm, not hysterical, good-old-Tommy 'fan' cheers, or a salute to any average lounge-set, but the crash of applause from an audience that is delighted, and sometimes stirred profoundly.

'That kind of cheering followed the fall of the Stratford-upon-Avon curtain on John Gielguld's revival of *Much Ado About Nothing* ... John Gielgud's Benedick woos us in festival terms. His return to full stature as a Shakespearean has lodged the season safely in the records. .... It was an evening of clear excitement. Now that Benedick is back in Gielgud's repertory, he should remain there.'

And remain there he did for several years. Gielgud played him again in London in 1952 with Diana Wynyard as Beatrice; in London and on the continent in 1955 with Peggy Ashcroft, and finally in the United States in 1959 with Margaret Leighton.

Much Ado About Nothing

Left: with Peggy Ashcroft on the European tour in 1955. According to Gielgud, she played the part 'almost with a touch of Beatrice Lillie . . . and created a cheeky character who means well but seems to drop bricks all the time (perhaps she got it from me).'
Below: with Diana Wynyard as Beatrice, Phoenix Theatre, 1952.
Right: with Peggy Ashcroft at Stratford in 1950, with a fine cast that included Robert Shaw and Alan Badel.

Maxine Audley as Mariana and John Gielgud as Angelo, in Measure for Measure, *Stratford, 1950.*

Thanks to Gielgud's presence at the head of the company and to his potency at the box office, the 1950 season at Stratford began a month earlier than in previous years. The opening production was Peter Brook's *Measure for Measure* in which Gielgud gave a haunting, steel-hard portrayal of Angelo, 'discovering new depths of feeling and ranges of voice' (T. C. Worsley) in an unromantic role that a few years before he might have felt was too unsympathetic for him to want to tackle.

After *Much Ado* the third production was *Julius Caesar*, directed by Michael Langham and Anthony Quayle, who also played Mark Antony, with Andrew Cruickshank as Caesar, Harry Andrews as Brutus and Gielgud playing against his instinct as a hard-edged, embittered and knowing Cassius. 'The performance of the season,' J. C. Trewin called it, 'and – I would say – the Shakespearean performance of the year.'

Opposite: Gielgud's second assault on King Lear, *at the Old Vic, 1940.*

Gielgud's final appearance that season was less sure-footed, at least at the opening. J. C. Trewin again: 'On the first night it seemed that Gielgud's King Lear had not grown since the Vic revival of 1940: until near the end the actor, intellectually commanding, illuminated the part from without rather than from within: he was slow in developing pathos, though once the première was over his grip on the part strengthened.'

Fortunately, one or two of the critics went twice and the Lear they saw the second time round displayed none of the initial uncertainties. According to T. C. Worsley, 'In the first we were conscious of Mr Gielgud acting: we admired the grasp, the range, the subtlety, the sureness, the intellectual force, the largeness. In the second . . . this seemed not acting – something conscious and willed – but the actual enacting itself of events seen for the first (and only) time, into the heart of which we ourselves are led, stumbling with the old king down the deep descent.'

Gielgud played Lear for the third time in a production he co-directed with Anthony Quayle at Stratford, 1950. Opposite: the 'Japanese' Lear, co-directed with Peter Brook, designed by Isamu Nogushi, 1955.

All in all, it had been an extraordinary season for Gielgud, one, as Richard Findlater noted at the time, that 'had deepened and widened his acting range, ripening his fine sensibility, intelligence and skill', and one that had given him renewed confidence in his powers and a new awareness of his inner strengths and potential.

With the exception of *Julius Caesar*, which the public had enjoyed, but which he and the company claimed to have been ill-at-ease with, Gielgud had found the season satisfying as well as stimulating. He had particularly enjoyed working with the young Peter Brook – 'He was awfully clever at knowing when I was false. One wants to be told when one is bad and false, but one doesn't want to be put down so that one loses confidence' – and renewed his association with him the following year when he played Leontes in Brook's Festival of Britain production of *The Winter's Tale*. Gielgud sensed that Leontes might offer him similar opportunities to those he had exploited so effectively as Angelo. Leontes and Angelo are not evil figures bereft of all moral sense (unlike Iago, which Gielgud never played, or Ferdinand in *The*

Julius Caesar*: Gielgud as Cassius with Michael Gwynn as Casca and Percy Herbert as Cinna, Stratford, 1950.*

The Winter's Tale, *1951, directed by Peter Brook. Overleaf: assisted by his dresser, 'Mac', John Gielgud changes and makes up for the role of Leontes.*

Duchess of Malfi, which he clearly did not enjoy), but real people with all the failings and frailities of humanity. To Gielgud the parts offered not only opportunities for creating subtle psychological portraits, but also effective theatre: 'Angelo and Leontes . . . are both given wonderful scenes of repentance in which they are shamed, humiliated and at last forgiven. These later scenes give a fine opportunity for the actor to show both sides of the character.'

Gielgud took that opportunity and enjoyed another success that confirmed that, at forty-seven, he was again at the height of his considerable powers. After visiting the Edinburgh Festival, *The Winter's Tale* moved to the Phoenix for a record-breaking run where John followed it up with the revival of *Much Ado*. Next he returned to Stratford to direct Ralph Richardson in an unhappy production of *Macbeth* (Kenneth Tynan was 'unmoved to the point of paralysis' and sadly he was not alone) before flying off to Hollywood to recreate his Cassius in Joseph Mankiewicz's film of *Julius Caesar*.

PHOENIX THEATRE
TEM. 8611
CHARING CROSS ROAD, W.C.2
Licensed by the Lord Chamberlain to Prince Littler

EVENINGS (Mon. to Fri.) 7.30 sharp   SAT. 5 & 8.30
Matinee: WED. at 2.30

TENNENT PRODUCTIONS Ltd.
(in association with the Arts Council of Great Britain)
present

JOHN GIELGUD   DIANA WYNYARD

AND

FLORA ROBSON

in

THE WINTER'S TALE
by WILLIAM SHAKESPEARE

GEORGE HOWE		GEORGE ROSE
Brewster Mason	Charles Doran	Kenneth Edwards
Hazel Terry	Charlotte Mitchell	Joy Rodgers
MICHAEL GOODLIFFE		PHILIP GUARD
John Moffat	Philip Pearman	Paul Hardwick
Michael Nightingale	Hugh Stewart	Denys Graham
VIRGINIA McKENNA		RICHARD GALE
Frances Hyland	Sarah Davies	Margaret Wolfit
William Patrick	Oliver Cox	Norman Bird
Churton Fairman	Robert Anderson	Donald Hindle
	and	

LEWIS CASSON

> **Directed by PETER BROOK**
> Decor by SOPHIE FEDOROVITCH
> Music by CHRISTOPHER FRY

John Gielgud and Diana Wynyard as Leontes and Hermione in *The Winter's Tale*
(Photo: Angus McBean)

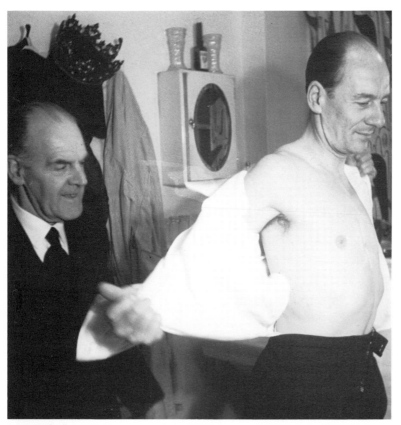

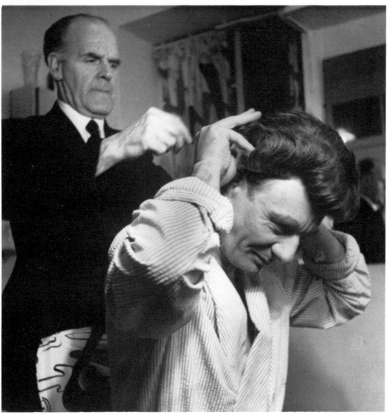

Opposite: on stage as Leontes, with Robert Anderson as Mamillius.

Gielgud returned to London in the autumn of 1952 with plans for a season of three plays to be presented by the Tennent management at the Lyric, Hammersmith. *Vogue* magazine was among those that looked forward to the event with relish: 'John Gielgud, the nonpareil, the cynosure of the theatre, is the flashing, sparkling mind behind this new season of such infinite promise – he will direct three plays, acts himself in the second and third. Now his powers are at their greatest – sensibility, strength, imagination, wit, combined to make the true aristocrat of both tragedy and comedy.'

Richard II was to be the opening production and Gielgud had contemplated returning to the role himself, but resisted the temptation, feeling he would now be thought too old for the part and giving it instead to Paul Scofield who had just turned thirty and who made a success of it under John's direction, despite the difficulty of working with a director who clearly still felt the part to be his own.

Programmes from the Gielgud Season at the Lyric, Hammersmith, 1953.

The Lyric season's second offering was Congreve's *The Way of the World*. A few critics cavilled at Pamela Brown's Millament,

but most agreed with Tynan that Gielgud had produced a sparkling revival: 'Having assembled what I heard described, in an enviable slip of the tongue, as "a conglamouration of stars," he has let them have their heads. The play sails into life with pennants flying. Mr Gielgud is at the helm, a crowd of deft character actors like Eric Porter, Richard Wordsworth, and Brewster Mason are manning the rigging, and Eileen Herlie is thrown in for ballast. To pipe us aboard there is Paul Scofield as Witwould, the amateur fop – a beautifully gaudy performance, pitched somewhere between Hermione Gingold and Stan Laurel. Gielgud's galleon would not be complete without a figurehead, and there, astride the prow, she triumphantly is – Margaret Rutherford, got up as Lady Wishfort, the man-hungry pythoness.'

The surprise of the season was Thomas Otway's *Venice Preserv'd*, regarded by many as the finest post-Jacobean tragedy and popular with leading actors from the time it was written in 1681 to the early nineteenth century, though little performed since. Gielgud hadn't seen the last major revival – in 1920, also at the Lyric Hammersmith – but he had read the play more than once and was confident it had potential. Peter Brook's production realised that potential and *Venice Preserv'd* with Gielgud and Scofield well matched in the two leading roles, was the critical success of the season – albeit the only play to lose money.

It was during the run of *Venice Preserv'd* – and thanks, in part, to personal representations made to the Prime Minister, Churchill, by Olivier and Richardson, both of whom had been knighted in 1947 – that Gielgud received the knighthood that so many of his colleagues and his public felt was long overdue. The recognition thrilled him, of course, and the ovation he received from the audience at the Lyric when the Coronation Honours List had just been announced touched him deeply. For once there was a fair excuse for the famous, freely-flowing Gielgud tears.

With his mother, Sir John Gielgud makes his first appearance as a Knight Bachelor after his investiture at Buckingham Palace on 29 June, 1953.

At the London Palladium on 28 May, 1953 in a 'Stars at Midnight' charity show, Laurence Olivier (knighted 1947), John Mills (knighted 1976) and John Gielgud (knighted 1953) sing 'Three Juvenile Delinquents' by Noël Coward (knighted 1970).

That summer, in Bulawayo, as part of the Rhodes Centenary Festival, Sir John bade a final farewell to one of his most cherished roles. He had badly wanted to play Richard II one last time, but he quickly realised it was a mistake. 'I was terribly disappointed to find that contrary to my expectations it gave me no joy at all. I could only imitate the performance I saw when I was a young man. And I thought, "No, I must leave this part alone because the fact that I am older and wiser doesn't make me better in the part. I just give an imitation of what I used to do and I did it better then because I was young." You can't imitate a young part with any pleasure.'

While he played it with great effect, there was not much real pleasure to be had from Gielgud's next role, that of the humour-less, fastidious prig Julian Anson in N. C. Hunter's *A Day by the Sea*. Gielgud had wanted to do a new play and had the option of the Hunter or of taking on John Whiting's much more complex and challenging *Marching Song*. Sir John went for the safer, softer option, and appeared with an all-star cast – Richardson, Sybil Thorndike, Lewis Casson, Irene Worth, Megs Jenkins – in what Tynan described as 'an evening of unexampled triviality', which was *exactly* what the public appeared to want. They flocked to the Haymarket.

1953, N. C. Hunter's A Day by the Sea.

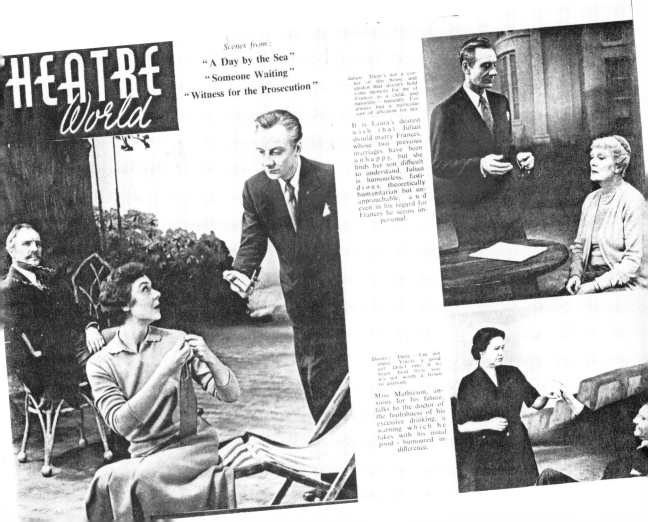

Scenes from:
"A Day by the Sea"
"Someone Waiting"
"Witness for the Prosecution"

Julian: There's not a corner of this house and garden that doesn't hold some memory for me of Frances as a child, and naturally — naturally I've always had a particular sort of affection for her.

It is Laura's dearest wish that Julian should marry Frances, whose two previous marriages have been unhappy, but she finds her son difficult to understand. Julian is humourless, fastidious, theoretically humanitarian but unapproachable, and even in his regard for Frances he seems impersonal.

Doctor: There I'm not angry. You're a good girl. Don't take it to heart. God bless you, it's not worth a frown to anybody.

Miss Mathieson, anxious for his future, talks to the doctor of the foolishness of his excessive drinking, a warning which he takes with his usual good-humoured indifference.

This was a difficult time for Gielgud personally and a tiring time for him professionally. While appearing in *A Day by the Sea*, he directed, first, a commercial pot-boiler in the form of *Charley's Aunt*, the Brandon Thomas farce in which he'd first appeared exactly forty years before, and then, at the Lyric, Hammersmith, his own adaptation – designed to make the dialogue more naturalistic and colloquial – of *The Cherry Orchard* with Trevor Howard and Gwen Ffrangcon-Davies. The strain told on him and he was taken ill, though the production did not appear to suffer. Noël Coward went to see it and was entranced: 'A magical evening in the theatre; every part subtly and perfectly played, and a beautiful production so integrated and timed that the heart melted. We came away prancing on the toes and very proud that we belonged to the theatre.'

The Gielgud make-up includes great resilience as well as vulnerability, and that resilience was needed in 1955 when, after directing a disappointing *Twelfth Night*, at Stratford with the Oliviers (Sir Laurence as Malvolio, Vivien Leigh doubling as Viola and Sebastian), he took on *King Lear* in a production that was dominated – swamped even – by the work of the Japanese designer Isamu Noguchi. In the programme Gielgud explained that the object had been 'to find a setting and costumes which would be free of historical or decorative associations so that the timeless, universal and mythical quality of the story may be clear . . .' In the event for many critics and most spectators the background was both too bizarre and too obtrusive, though for more than a few 'the greatness of Sir John's interpretation was not altogether dimmed.' Looking back on the 'great disaster' a decade later Gielgud was able to pinpoint where he felt he and his director had gone wrong: 'The great mistake I made in the Japanese *Lear* was a purely technical one. Noguchi, who is a sculptor, designed the sets and sent them to us and we thought they were thrilling and I still think they were, but I did not know at the time that he had never designed costumes. He arrived with no costumes, he designed them very hastily, he left before he had seen the fittings, he was not at the dress rehearsal or the first night. We all looked so strange and peculiar and I remember saying to George Devine who was directing the play: "Don't you think we could discard all the costumes and get some rubber sheets and make them into drapes and all wear sort of nondescript cloaks? I believe with this scenery that might work." And I still believe it might have done; but we hadn't the courage at the last moment to make such a drastic alteration, so I went through with it because I felt Noguchi was too individual and brilliant a designer to throw overboard completely, or half throw overboard which would be even more dishonest.'

The Japanese *Lear* – which, according to Gielgud, was admired by the young and the avant-garde and which Peter Brook acknowledged as the starting point for his own triumphant production with Paul Scofield eight years later – was coupled with the revival of *Much Ado about Nothing* and both played to packed houses in London and on two brief European tours. From

Shakespeare, Gielgud wanted to turn again to something modern and light. He settled on the part of the valet in Noël Coward's *Nude With Violin*. Coward had hoped for Rex Harrison and accepted Gielgud as an alternative with a little reluctance. In November 1955 he confided to his diary, 'Binkie is very keen for Johnny Gielgud to play *Nude with Violin* and so, although I do not think him ideal, I have consented. He is a star and a box-office draw, and although his comedy is a bit heavy-handed his quality will be valuable. Fortunately there is no love element and no emotion in the part, and if he plays it down, as I have implored him to do, he will probably, with a strong cast round him, make a success of it.'

He did indeed. In general the notices were dire, and in particular Tynan was at his most vitriolic ('Sir John never acts seriously in modern dress; it is the lounging attire in which he relaxes between classical bookings; and his present performance as a simpering valet is an act of boyish mischief, carried out with extreme elegance and the general aspect of a tight, smart, walking umbrella'), but the public paid no attention and turned up at the Globe Theatre in droves.

Nicky Edmett, John Gielgud and Joyce Carey in Nude with Violin, *1956.*

The Tempest

'Prospero has long been a favourite of mine.' Above: with Doreen Aris as Miranda in Peter Brooks' 1957 production. Left: the 1940 production at the Old Vic, directed by George Devine and Marius Goring. Right: Peter Hall's National Theatre production, 1974.

Gielgud stayed in the play for nine months, only leaving when he was due to start rehearsals for Peter Brook's Stratford production of *The Tempest* in the Summer of 1957. This time he conceived Prospero as a character in a revenge play 'gradually being convinced that hatred and revenge are useless'. He played the role as a powerful but embittered aristocrat, with concentrated anger and anguish, 'his face all rigour and pain, his voice all cello and woodwind' (Tynan) and many regarded it as the definitive Prospero. When it transferred to London it filled the vast Theatre Royal, Drury Lane, for sixty-one performances.

A year later Gielgud returned to Shakespeare and to the Old Vic for his first appearance in *Henry VIII*. Given his physique and *timbre*, he was unlikely casting for Cardinal Wolsey and while the big scene that depicts the Cardinal's downfall – the moment that had drawn Gielgud to the play – was played with poignancy (and Gielgud tears), the Tynan verdict was endorsed by many: 'Though Sir John made good use of his poker back and doorknob face, he never for a moment suggested Wolsey the self-made "butcher's cur"; all was rigid declamation, issuing from a tense and meagre tenor.'

His return to Stratford and his next untried Shakespeare was even less successful. *Othello*, directed by Franco Zeffirelli, with Sir John as the Moor, Ian Bannen as Iago, Dorothy Tutin as Desdemona and Peggy Ashcroft as Emilia, fell victim to one of those disastrous first nights – complete with cumbersome costumes, shaky scenery and half-remembered lines – that are sometimes entertaining to hear about, but always agony to

1961: Franco Zeffirelli directs Othello. 'He wasn't able to give me – or Peggy Ashcroft either – the right sort of confidence. We both suffered bitterly although we were both devoted to him and he had the most boundless universal charm.'

endure. While several of Gielgud's colleagues and one or two of the critics sensed the potential of a great performance, the production was reckoned a failure. 'This was a bitter blow to me,' he confessed a year or two later, 'because I've wanted all my life to play Othello, although I'm quite sure the public would never think me a satisfactory Othello in every way because I haven't got what Agate used to call the thew and sinew.'

Though utterly charmed by Zeffirelli as a man, Gielgud's confidence in him as a director never became established: 'Zeffirelli made the fatal mistake of dressing me as a Venetian, so that I looked, as many of the notices said, like an Indian Civil Servant. I didn't stand out from the others. Desdemona was over-dressed, I was under-dressed, there was much too much scenery, there were I think very damaging cuts, and certain other members of the cast were to my mind fatal. And it was terribly badly lit, which was very strange for Zeffirelli. He had dark scenery, so that with my dark face and dark clothes people couldn't see me – and when

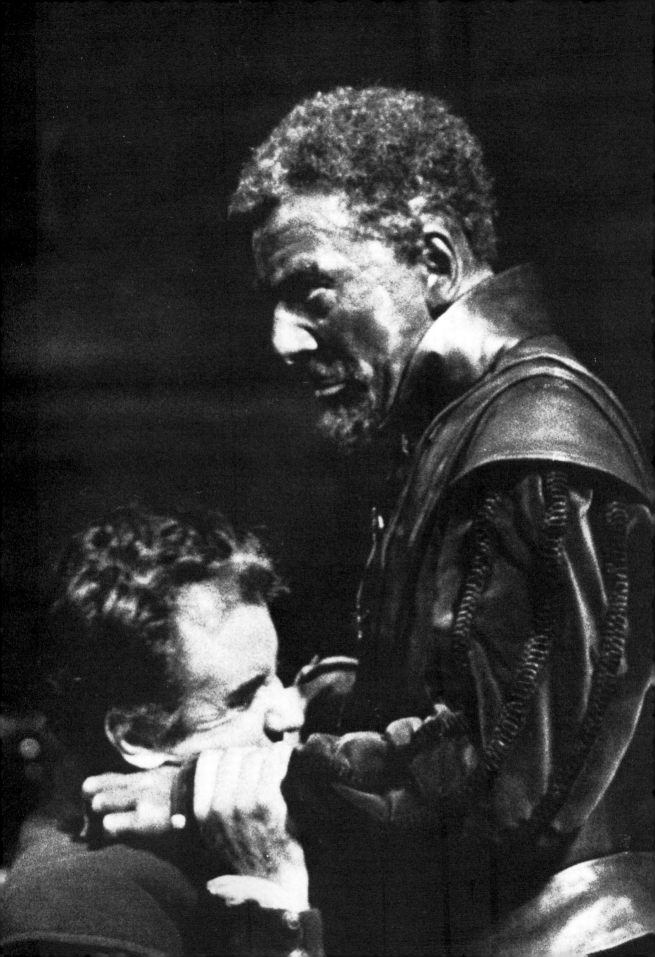

Opposite: Gielgud as Othello, Ian Bannen as Iago, Stratford, 1961.

one feels one is not well lit, one is immediately at a disadvantage. He also did some terribly dangerous things like putting me far too much upstage; he had a wonderful-looking scene with a huge table and imprisoned me behind it so I couldn't get any contact with the audience or with the other actors.'

However Gielgud was to enjoy a Shakespearean success at this time, not in any play, but in his one-man show based on George Rylands' Shakespeare anthology *The Ages of Man*. The solo recital was given its first public showing at the Edinburgh Festival in September 1957, followed by a brief European tour. A year later

Having toured in Britain, the United States and Canada in 1957 and 1958, Gielgud's Shakespearean recital comes to the West End in the summer of 1959.

Sir John took it on a more extensive tour of Canada and the United States and then on to Broadway, where it won great acclaim. Even the often grudging Kenneth Tynan, while repeating his line that 'Gielgud is the finest actor on earth from the neck up,' conceded that it was one of the 'most satisfactory things' Gielgud had ever done. 'Poker-backed he may be; poker-faced he certainly isn't. Wherever pride, scorn, compassion, and the more cerebral kinds of agony are called for, his features respond promptly, and memorably.'

Not everyone found the solo recital equally satisfying, ('He was superb in his quiet moments, but not so good when he wept and roared' said Coward), but it provided Sir John with a perfect vehicle for his unique vocal virtuosity and he was to perform it, off and on, around the world for several years to come.

Shortly before he set off for the first American tour of *The Ages of Man*, his mother died at the age of eighty-nine. A couple of years later, in an interview he gave in New York, he talked about the solo recital and the way the use of personal images had helped him in performance: 'When my mother died two years ago – I had never seen anyone dead before – it naturally made a tremendous impression upon me, and at a certain moment when I was doing the recital which came soon afterwards, in the "To be or not to be" speech, on a certain line, I always thought of her, of exactly how she looked when she was dead. It came into my mind, it didn't hold me up, but it gave me exactly the right feeling of the voice for the line. It came to me naturally, you know, without knowing it the first time, and it was so vivid that I thought I could never speak the speech again without thinking of it, because it would help me to make the line right, and it always did.'

'You've already shown me that - now show me something else'

For ten years, between 1957 and 1967, John Gielgud performed *The Ages of Man* around the globe, from Ireland to the Soviet Union, from the West End to Broadway. As a solo performer of Shakespeare he enjoyed an enviable success wherever he went. As an actor, over the same period, his fortunes were more mixed,

In 1961 he returned to one of his great loves, Chekhov, and received warm praise for his endearing, self-mocking portrayal of Gaev in *The Cherry Orchard*. This was a Royal Shakespeare Company production, directed by Michel Saint-Denis with Peggy Ashcroft as Madame Ranevsky and almost as long a rehearsal period as they had enjoyed when the three of them had last worked together on *The Three Sisters* in 1938. *The Cherry Orchard* did not achieve the same extraordinary success, but Gielgud found his part 'delightfully rewarding'; it 'suited me, I think, better than any other in which Saint-Denis has directed me; at least I enjoyed working for him more on this occasion than ever before.'

He turned again to Chekhov in 1965, when he directed and played the title role in the commercial West End première of *Ivanov*. Sir John had admired the play ever since he has seen it – his first Chekhov – directed by Komisarjevsky in 1925, and gave it a thoughtful and loving production that many critics found uneven and some found laboured. In London it was not unsuc-

Previous page: directing The Trojans *at Covent Garden, 1957.*

cessful, but in 1966 in New York, with Vivien Leigh replacing Yvonne Mitchell as Anna Petrovna, the press were less generous and business was poor.

Much more solidly successful on both sides of the Atlantic was Gielgud's revival of *The School for Scandal* in 1962. With a starry cast – Richardson, Margaret Rutherford, John Neville, Daniel Massey, Anna Massey – he directed the play with predictable polish at the Haymarket and then took over from John Neville as Joseph Surface before the whole production moved to Canada and the United States where it played to excellent business and enthusiastic notices. Gielgud's Joseph Surface was considered the 'very model' of how the part should be played: stylish, incisive, perfectly timed, impeccably phrased.

The triumphs, however, were matched by disasters, and these all seem to be in new plays. Gielgud hadn't yet discovered the knack – or simply had the luck – of finding original work by contemporary writers that both appealed to the public and suited his temperament and talent. In Graham Greene's *The Potting Shed*, as the over-wrought James Callifer, a traumatised figure from Greene's gallery of whisky priests, Gielgud has several moving moments (when he was able to shed real Terry tears) but he was ill at ease in the play and, with exceptions, the critics found both the piece and the performance unconvincing.

Opposite: with Peggy Ashcroft and Dorothy Tutin in The Cherry Orchard, *Aldwych, 1961, and below, with Gwen Ffrangcon-Davies in* The Potting Shed, *Globe, 1958.*

In 1960 at the Phoenix Gielgud and Richardson teamed up
to appear in Enid Bagnold's latest offering *The Last Joke*. This time
the critics were derisive, the audience jeered and the run was brief.
Jerome Kilty's dramatisation of Thornton Wilder's *The Ides of
March* at the Haymarket in 1963 – with Gielgud as Julius Caesar
togged up in a lounge suit and shortie toga to create an uncomfortable ancient-cum-modern dress – was given a similar critical
mauling. Again the audience booed. In Edward Albee's play *Tiny
Alice*, on Broadway, at the end of 1964, audiences and critics were
both bewildered and frustrated. Noël Coward saw it and reported
to his diary: 'The first act was hopeful, after that a chaotic mess
of sex and symbolism. Beautifully directed and acted except for
poor Johnny G. who was strained and unconvincing. Altogether
a maddening evening in the theatre, so nearly good and yet so
bloody pretentious.'

This was a bitter disappointment to Gielgud who yearned for
a success in a contemporary play and battled heroically to make
the Albee work. The film critic Stanley Kauffmann saw the play
and gave a chilling account of Sir John's lone struggle against

1960: with Ralph Richardson in The
Last Joke.

the odds in the closing minutes of the play: 'Through the evening Gielgud and his colleagues had done their best with this spurious work but had progressively lost the audience. Then he was left alone – deserted, one could say – to finish, in a torrent of fevered rhetoric, a play that had long ceased to matter. The audience began to murmur and rustle as he kept on and on. The buzz swelled a bit, punctuated by giggles. Toward the end he seemed isolated, separated by an invisible wall of protest. I was filled with admiration, not because of any "show must go on" hokum but at his power of concentration, his inner ear. He had kept his own music going against a hostile chorus.'

1963: with John Stride in The Ides of March.

His debut with the National Theatre in the 1967/8 season was unlucky too. As Orgon in Tyrone Guthrie's production of Molière's *Tartuffe*, Sir John was the victim both of improbable casting and of an uneven production that never seemed to get the balance of the piece quite right. And again with Peter Brook's version of Seneca's *Oedipus*, while Gielgud gave what Olivier described as 'a perfect tragic performance', it was in the uncertain context of a controversial production that some found austere and unremitting and others awkward and eccentric.

These were not the best of years for Gielgud the actor, nor even for Gielgud the director, because, of course, when he was not performing in a play he was directing one. From his first production of *Romeo and Juliet* for the OUDS in 1932 ('fresh and clean' Harcourt Williams had called it) to his last West End Offering in 1975 (a disappointing revival of Pinero's *The Gay Lord Quex*), Gielgud

Above: in December 1932 Gielgud directed the Old Vic Company in The Merchant of Venice.

Left: in January 1932 he made his debut as a director with a production for the Oxford University Dramatic Society of Romeo and Juliet *with Christopher Hassall and Peggy Ashcroft.*

was responsible for more than sixty productions and the range of work was immense: Shakespeare, Chekhov, the classics, flimsy potboilers, quality revivals, worthy middle-of-the-road commercial plays suitable for 'canopy names' to star in, even grand opera: at Covent Garden in 1957 he directed the first English professional stage performance of Berlioz's *The Trojans*; in 1961, again at Covent Garden, with Solti conducting and spellbinding designs by John Piper, he produced the first London performance of Benjamin Britten's *A Midsummer Night's Dream*; and in 1968 he was responsible for the *Don Giovanni* at the London Coliseum.

John Gielgud directs opera – opposite, with Blanche Thebom in her dressing room at Covent Garden for The Trojans *in 1957, and below, one of 'John Piper's scenes of breathtaking loveliness' in* A Midsummer Night's Dream.

Royal Opera House
COVENT GARDEN

THE ROYAL OPERA HOUSE, COVENT GARDEN LIMITED
GENERAL ADMINISTRATOR · DAVID L. WEBSTER
HOUSE MANAGER · JOHN COLLINS

presents

the first English professional stage performance of

THE TROJANS

OPERA IN FIVE ACTS

Music by HECTOR BERLIOZ
Text by the composer after Virgil

English text by E. J. DENT

Scenery and Costumes by MARIANO ANDREU

Choreography by MERIEL EVANS

CONDUCTOR — RAFAEL KUBELIK

PRODUCER — JOHN GIELGUD

THURSDAY, 6th JUNE, 1957
at 6 p.m.

Royal Opera House
COVENT GARDEN
HOUSE MANAGER   JOHN COLLINS

THE ROYAL OPERA HOUSE, COVENT GARDEN LIMITED

GENERAL ADMINISTRATOR · SIR DAVID WEBSTER
ASSISTANT GENERAL ADMINISTRATOR · JOHN TOOLEY

in association with the Arts Council of Great Britain

presents

THE COVENT GARDEN OPERA

in

the first London performance of

Midsummer Night's Dream

OPERA IN THREE ACTS

Music by BENJAMIN BRITTEN

Libretto after WILLIAM SHAKESPEARE
by PETER PEARS *and* BENJAMIN BRITTEN

Conductor : GEORG SOLTI

Producer : JOHN GIELGUD

Scenery and costumes by JOHN PIPER
Costume Assistant: Alan Pickford
Mr. Piper acknowledges the help of Carl Toms

Lighting by WILLIAM BUNDY

THURSDAY, 2nd FEBRUARY, 1961

John Gielgud and Georg Solti, director and conductor of the first London performance of Benjamin Britten's A Midsummer Night's Dream.

With so much work over so many years, inevitably the quality was variable, but from start to finish Gielgud the director was known for one besetting sin: the constant changeability of his quicksilver mind. In 1938, writing about Gielgud as both actor and director, Michel Saint-Denis observed, 'When one sees Gielgud, it does not take long to discover that he is restless, anxious, nervous and impressionable. He is not over-confident in himself. His restlessness goes with a tendency to be dissatisfied. Therefore he works out more and more plans, more and more ideas, rejecting one for another, working all the time from instinct rather than from careful study.'

In any memoir of what it is like working with Gielgud the director's complaints about this restless quest for something new and different come up again and again. At the start of rehearsals the incessant changes can be stimulating and inventive: as the first night nears they become alarming.

Cecil Beaton on *Lady Windermere's Fan* in 1945: 'Lady Windermere has opened to excellent notices on its trial trip to the provinces. All portends well: it has been a comparatively smooth

Opposite: Gielgud the director at rehearsal for Crisis in Heaven *at the Lyric in 1944.*

undertaking. Few major alterations have had to be made although until the last minute John Gielgud continued to change his direction.'

Laurence Olivier recalling *Twelfth Night* in 1955: 'He still had the disconcerting habit of changing moves at every single rehearsal; of course a director has the right to change his mind, but after almost four weeks and with the opening night looming closer, I began to be nervous that the occasion would be a shambles, with an utterly confused company knowing neither the timing nor the placing of the moves. Noël Coward once said that the only real use of a director was to stop the actors from bumping into each other; at the rate our *Twelfth Night* was going our first performance would have been more like a game of Blind Man's Buff than anything else.'

Coward himself on *Nude with Violin* in 1956: 'John has directed the play with loving care and reverence and given everyone so much fussy business to do that most of the comedy lines are lost.

With Noël Coward in Dublin during the pre-London run of Nude with Violin, *October 1956.*

They get up, sit down, carry trays in and out, change places and move around so incessantly that I nearly went out of my mind. . . . It is extraordinary that a fine director like Johnny, who can do *The Cherry Orchard* and *A Day by the Sea* so superbly, should have gone so very far wrong. I can only conclude that it was over-anxiety.'

Much of Gielgud's work as a director since the war – from *The Heiress* with Ashcroft and Richardson in 1949, when he was brought in at the last minute and performed a radical rescue job, to a pleasing *Private Lives* with Maggie Smith and Robert Stephens in 1972 – has been successful: clear-cut, well-orchestrated and stylish. Some of the productions were too busy, fussy and confused – Terence Rattigan's relatively successful *Variations on a Theme* (1958) was one, M. J. Farrell and John Perry's disastrous *Dazzling Prospect* (1961) another – but many more – *The Chalk Garden* (1956), *Five Finger Excercise* (1958), *Half Way Up the Tree* (1967) – were the reliable work of a seasoned craftsman.

In 1963 Gielgud defined the qualities he regarded as essential to a Shakespearean director: '. . . industry, patience . . . sensitivity, originality without freakishness, a fastidious ear and eye, some respect for, and knowledge of, tradition, a feeling for music and pictures, colour and design; yet in none of these, I believe, should he be too opinionated in his views and tastes. For a theatrical production, at every stage of its preparation, is always changing, unpredictable in its moods and crises.'

A year later he directed his own last Shakespearean production: *Hamlet* on Broadway with Richard Burton. The reviews were mixed, but the receipts were fabulous and the production ran for 138 performances, breaking John's own record by six performances. The Burton-Gielgud collaboration attracted a mass of publicity, a ton of newsprint and at least two full-length blow-by-blow accounts of the making of the production. In one, William Redfield, the actor playing Guildenstern, revealed that he and others in the cast were alarmed to find that Gielgud as a director didn't concern himself with 'the play's circumstances but only with its effects.' Gielgud quoted his old mentor Harley Granville-Barker to them in an attempt to encourage them to pace, shape and colour their performance rather than relying exclusively on circumstance and absolute psychological truth. 'Granville-Barker once said to me, "You've already shown me that – now show me something else." It was a wonderful direction for me because I tend to be monotonous. After that, I always made sure that each scene I played had a different colour, a new shape. Even the lines should change every few moments or so. If I do one line this way, then the next should be that way and then the next should change and the next. It's good to keep the audience off balance, you know – always interested – perhaps even a bit confused.'

Naturally, as he admitted in another interview, with actors of the first rank, his approach is far less didactic: 'If I direct a play with wonderful actors, I know that my work will not be as difficult or will not be the same as when I get an ordinary cast of fairly good actors. I mean, if you get Peggy Ashcroft and Edith Evans,

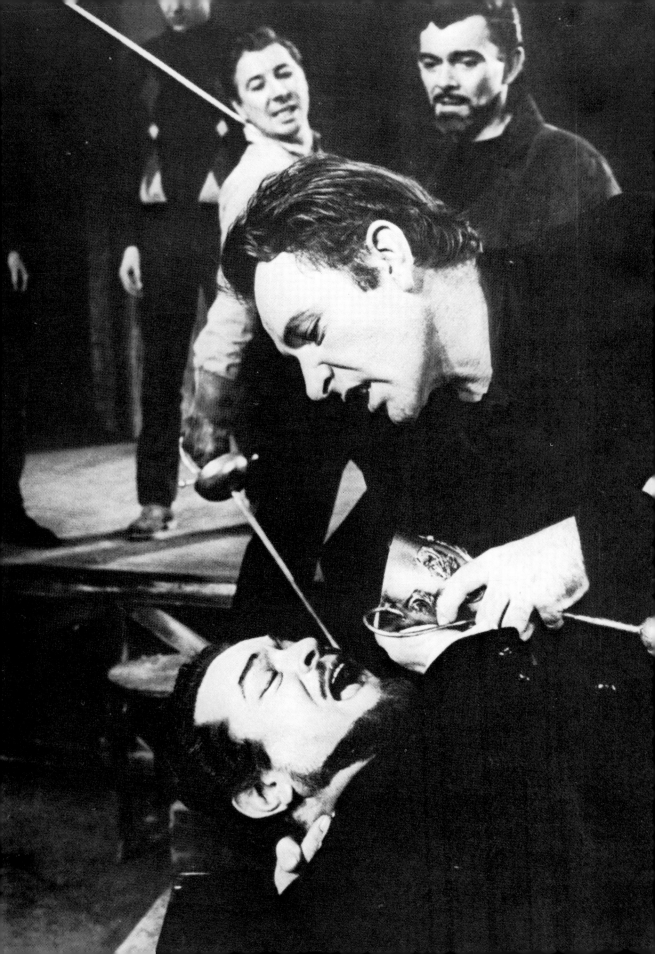

Hamlet

John Gielgud's production with Richard Burton as Hamlet, and Alfred Drake as Claudius (opposite), at the Lunt-Fontanne Theater, New York, April 1964, the quatercentenary of Shakespeare's birth. Above, from left to right: Gielgud (director and the voice of the Ghost of Hamlet's father), Richard Sterne (A Gentleman), Richard Burton (Hamlet) and Robert Milli (Horatio).

as I had in *The Chalk Garden*, I say that I just put up the tennis net and clear the court and act as referee, because they know much more about what they want to do than I do. I'm only there as a kind of audience to check the spacing, the movement, the pace of the play. You can't really direct people who are enormously talented, I don't think.'

But you can try. The only time Gielgud and Richardson had any serious difference of opinion in a production was when Sir John was directing Sir Ralph in *The School for Scandal* and they couldn't agree over Richardson's first crucial entrance as Sir Peter Teazle. 'Ralph argued every day and we could not begin to rehearse the scene. "Should I have a newspaper in my hand? A walking stick? Or be taking snuff perhaps?" At last one morning he leaned across the footlights and said, "You know, Johnnie, I prayed to God last night to tell me how to come in this opening scene. And this morning God answered, 'Do what it says in the text, just come on'"'.'

Much of Gielgud's best work as a director was in plays in which he appeared himself. Being both director and star is a risky combination: 'People are always saying they think it's not a good plan; my most intimate friends have always counselled me against it, and thought I took on too much. There's no doubt that I did overtax my strength very often.'

One of the great advantages of a director being in his own production, of course, is that he is there at every performance: 'After the play has opened, if I've only directed it, I come back every six or eight weeks to see it, and I find things have slipped and gone wrong, and I go back and see the actors and they're very hurt. They say, "Oh, we've been working very hard, while you were sitting at home drawing the money, and why should you tick us off, we've made this pause and it's so effective, and we get a big laugh on this line." If you complain about these things they take it rather badly and it's hard to make them rehearse well. But if you're in the play yourself, you can, two or three times a week, send little notes down, or you can rehearse a little bit before the play begins, or a little bit after, or you can go over something yourself, or you can talk to the person you're acting a scene with.'

The real danger of the director-star role in Gielgud's case was that too often he would concentrate on the production as a whole to the detriment of his personal performance. He gave his first energies to the rest of the company, leaving a full consideration of his own role till last: 'When I go on the road before we come to London, I get all the players as good as I can, and I put my own part in really as a sketch: it's rather hard on the audience, and perhaps on the actors too. But I keep on making my understudy walk for me, and when we've been on the road for a few weeks, I have another rehearsal and I make the understudy walk my whole part. I remember this worked extremely well, particularly in *The Lady's Not for Burning*, *Ivanov*, and *Much Ado*, and certainly in *Love for Love*; because I was able, after a few weeks, to see exactly where my part belonged, in the pattern, and drop into it to complete the picture, like the missing piece of a jigsaw puzzle.'

'New notes from an old cello'

In 1958 Gielgud was asked to play in the British première of Samuel Beckett's *Endgame*. He turned the offer down: 'I couldn't find anything that I liked in the play. I thought it's no good pretending for pretension's sake that I would play this play, because it nauseates me. I hate it and I won't play it, and yet I long to be in something as avant-garde as that.'

As the fifties gave way to the sixties, Gielgud began to regret the way he had publicly expressed his lack of sympathy with the new writers, began to envy an actor like Olivier who had risked going to the Royal Court and playing in Osborne and Ionesco, began to feel that he was becoming 'old hat' while being unsure of what could be done about it.

This sense of being out of touch, unable to relate to the writers of his time, lasted for several frustrating and unnerving years, until in 1968, at the age of sixty-four, he accepted the part of the Headmaster in Alan Bennett's play-cum-revue *Forty Years On*, and gave a witty, assured, self-mocking performance that was to earn him his best notices in a decade. *Forty Years On* was no dustbin drama, no existential piece of the absurd, but a nostalgic

Left: The Headmaster in Forty Years On *at the Apollo, 1968.*

Overleaf: with Irene Worth in Oedipus *at the Old Vic, 1968. With Patrick Magee in* The Battle of Shrivings *at the Lyric, 1970. With Ralph Richardson in* Home *at the Royal Court, 1970.*

Previous page: Gielgud's most recent stage appearance, as Sir Noel Cunliffe in Half-Life *at the Duke of York's, 1978.*

Opposite: Orgon in Tartuffe *with the National Theatre Company at the Old Vic, 1967.*

Opposite: Julius Caesar in Bernard Shaw's Caesar and Cleopatra, *Chichester Festival Theatre, 1971.*

pastiche – yet it was the vehicle that brought Gielgud back into the vanguard, that suddenly made him seem in no way a man out of his times but rather the complete contemporary.

Over the next ten years Gielgud was to take on a whole series of demanding roles by new and 'difficult' writers and to do so with a confidence and ease that would have suggested to someone who had not known of his career before the late sixties that here was an actor who was a natural frontiersman. The parts themselves were varied: Sir Gordon Petrie, the Bertrand Russell figure in Peter Shaffer's word-blown *The Battle of the Shrivings*; Harry, one of the patients in the mental home in David Storey's elliptical masterpiece *Home*; Sir Geoffrey Kendle, an hilarious caricature of Gielgud himself in *Veterans*, Charles Wood's comedy born out of his experience as scriptwriter for the film of *The Charge of the Light Brigade* in which Sir John had played Lord Raglan; Shakespeare in despairing and embittered old age in Edward Bond's *Bingo*; Spooner, the down-at-heel Bohemian writer manqué in Harold Pinter's elusive *tour de force No Man's Land*; Sir Noel Cunliffe, the elderly acidic archaeologist in Julian Mitchell's morbid *Half-Life*.

As Sir Geoffrey Kendle in Veterans, *Royal Court, 1972, and below with John Mills as Mr Laurence D'Orsay, as seen by Hewison in* Punch.

These were all uncompromising pieces of their time – and three of them were presented at the Royal Court, a theatre at which Gielgud would have felt sadly out of place a decade before – but in between playing the 'moderns' he did not altogether eschew the classics. He played Julius Caesar twice: at the Chichester Festival Theatre for Robin Phillips in a stylised and uneven production of Shaw's *Caesar and Cleopatra*, and at the National Theatre for John Schlesinger in Shakespeare's *Julius Caesar*. At the National too he worked with Peter Hall. They had been acquainted since the fifties – and Hall had offered to redirect the failed Zefferelli *Othello* in 1961 – but they hadn't worked together until *The Battle of the Shrivings*. Now they became close colleagues and Hall's diaries of the period are full of delightful insights to Gielgud's character. In 1977 Sir John played Sir Politick Would-be in Ben Jonson's *Volpone*. The production was lack-lustre but Gielgud's eccentric performance endearing. During one rehearsal Hall mentioned something about the dangers of over-playing. Gielgud blushed: 'Will I never learn? Still my old tricks after years and years and years: anything for a laugh, and because of that I don't get it.'

Gielgud's tendency to come up with a dozen ideas a minute – many of them mutually contradictory – was undiminished too. In *The Tempest* in 1973 Hall planned to present the play as a masque with Gielgud's Prospero dressed up in the style of the Elizabethan wizard Dr John Dee. Gielgud had his doubts. 'JG began the afternoon by announcing that he didn't want to wear a beard or hat or be in grey or black as Prospero, who was a boring man, and it was a boring part, and he didn't want to look boring. He questioned practically everything that I proposed . . . JG remembered that when he first played *The Tempest*, it was all divinely Eastern and he wore a turban. In a later production, he recalled, he wore a long grey beard and glasses. Then in Peter Brook's he had some kind of ragged, hermity shift with sandals. At the end of three hours, I had gently but firmly ridden John to a standstill and managed to get him to listen to why I was doing the play

Above: in 1974, Gielgud the campaigner, leading a delegation of actors – including Edward Woodward, Richard Briers, Fenella Fielding and Miriam Karlin – on a mission 'to save London theatres' and signing a petition on behalf of the Russian dancers Valery and Galina Panov.

Opposite: in 1974, Gielgud the actor, playing Shakespeare in Edward Bond's Bingo *at the Royal Court.*

in a Jacobean masque-like way. He then announced that he loved the set, and perhaps he had better wear a buttoned, belted, scholar's coat after all. And a beard (should he grow it or have a false one?) And he agreed to wear a scholar's hat. JG runs around in circles with huge charm and energy. He keeps making self-deprecating remarks, reminding us we shouldn't listen to him, and that he is a romantic who loves the old-fashioned theatre.'

Though he retained his reservations about his costume – and some about the production as a whole – Gielgud trusted and admired Hall. Judging from Hall's diaries the feeling was mutal: 'He is an amazing man, and my debt to him is enormous. He has never complained, never been restless. He has led the company and helped me every inch of the way.'

It was in Hall's production of the Pinter play *No Man's Land* that Gielgud enjoyed the outstanding success of his seventies. Once again his stage partner was his colleague and friend of fifty years standing, Ralph Richardson. When Lindsay Anderson brought them together as the two elderly mental hospital inmates in David Storey's *Home*, they had already played together on many occasions, but their work together now, in the Indian summer of their careers, seemed to have a magical dimension that their earlier stage encounters had lacked. As an American critic said, 'they simply make beautiful music together'. In *Home* it was in many ways the greater challenge for Gielgud since he had less to say, less to hold on to and work with. He had to ring the changes of colour, shape, tone, feeling, from a minimum of words, brief interjections, spasmodic sentences that trailed away, silences, but he did so with consummate technical expertise and breathtaking emotional force. Keith Dewhurst described the performance in *The Guardian*: 'Gielgud's weeping is a depth of emotion which he must find entirely within himself, since in the sense of story-line or interaction between the characters there is very little in the play to help him. . . . In *Home* the character just interrupts a conversation with tears and the way in which Gielgud does this, the way in which his whole face goes red and his eyes blink with salt, is simply an act of genius: a consummation of his lifetime's integrity.'

The success of *No Man's Land* – at the National, in the West End, on Broadway, on television – was prodigious. The moment Gielgud read the play he had known he wanted to do it. 'Peter Hall had sent the script to me expecting that I would want to play the "posh" part of Hirst, because it was more the kind of role I had done in the past. I told him "Don't be silly. The other part is infinitely more what I want to play." The part of Spooner was a complete impersonation, such as I had never had a chance to do in the theatre. It was very exciting to have a chance of doing it, and I was quick in finding a way to look and to dress. The moment I read the play I saw Spooner clearly, which was rare for me. I remember saying to Harold Pinter "I think Auden, don't you? Do you think sandals and socks?' and he jumped at the idea. Then I said, "Do you think we should add spectacles?' and he liked that too. About a week after we started rehearsal I came

Above and opposite: in performance and at rehearsal with Ian Charleson in Peter Hall's production of Volpone *at the National Theatre, 1977.*

Opposite, left to right: Ronald Pickup, Brian Cox, John Gielgud and Peter Needham in John Schlesinger's production of Julius Caesar *at the National Theatre, 1977.*

No Man's Land

Harold Pinter's compelling play was performed in London, in New York, and on television. 'I am proud and thrilled to feel that I have had not only a personal success but also a wonderful partnership with Ralph Richardson.'

In his seventies Gielgud suddenly found himself joining the awards ceremony and chat show circuit. Right, with Claire Bloom in 1976. Left, at the Evening Standard Drama Awards in 1980. Below, at the BBC in 1981. Along with all the awards and accolades, over the years Gielgud also managed to collect honorary degrees from the universities of Oxford, London and St Andrews, to become a Companion of the Légion d'Honneur and, in1977, to be made a Companion of Honour.

on the stage with a wig, the suit and the spectacles and everybody said "It's exactly right, perfect!" and I said, 'Yes, and now I must find a performance to go inside it."'

The performance he found – wry, sly, at moments ingratiating, at others vulnerable – was perfectly matched by Richardson's: they were a couple of masterly virtuosos at the height of their power. What the play was about – the no man's land between illusion and reality, between half-truth and self-awareness – was in some ways neither here nor there. As Gielgud said: 'why should the play "mean" anything if the audience was held the whole time and was never bored?'

For Gielgud it was an extraordinary experience: here he was in his mid-seventies, half a century and more after his London debut, enjoying a dazzling renaissance, being showered with awards and honours (he became a Companion of Honour in 1977) and more offers of work than he'd ever known. Because, as well as sustaining a career as a leading stage actor of unequalled length in the history of the theatre, he now emerged as one of the world's most sought-after film actors. In 1983, under the banner headline 'New Notes from an Old Cello', *Time* magazine ran a two-page spread on the phenomenon of the English actor who, in his eightieth year, had become 'the hottest young talent around':

Question: Is it possible to make a movies or TV series without John Gielgud?

Answer: Yes. But it is not easy.

Since 1980 his face has been seen on more screens than the MGM lion. Famous to serious theatregoers for more than 50 years, the reserved, sometimes frosty-appearing Gielgud has, in his 70s, suddenly assumed a new role – that of Major Movie Star.

Gielgud made his radio debut in 1923 and since then has appeared in scores of radio plays, both recreating many of his stage successes and appearing in new plays for the first time. He approached television more cautiously, making his first appearance in A Day by the Sea in 1959 with Gladys Cooper taking the role Sybil Thorndike had played on the stage with Gielgud in 1953. In the quarter century since his television debut, Gielgud has appeared on the small screen with increasing frequency.

Opposite: as the Mock Turtle in Jonathan Miller's production of Alice in Wonderland with Ann-Marie Mallik as Alice and Malcolm Muggeridge as the Gryphon, 1966. Right, above: as Lord Harry Wotton in John Osborne's adaptation of The Picture of Dorian Gray, 1976; and below: as Captain Shotover in Bernard Shaw's Heartbreak House, 1977.

John of Gaunt in Richard II, *1978, and below, the Grand Inquisitor in an episode from* The Brothers Karamazov, *1980.*

Opposite: In the television adaptation of Evelyn Waugh's novel, Brideshead Revisited, *directed by Charles Sturridge and Michael Lindsay Hogg, Gielgud's performance in the pivotal role of Edward Ryder, Charles Ryder's father, received universal acclaim.*

Most men retire at sixty-five, but that's when Gielgud's film career really began to take off and since then he has played in over thirty major films – good, bad and indifferent.

Gielgud made his film debut in the 1920s in a couple of silent pictures; the first a French melodrama *Who is the Man?* (originally written as a stage piece for Sarah Bernhardt by her godson) in which he played a neurotic sculptor and morphine addict, the second an Edgar Wallace thriller, *The Clue of the New Pin* in which he was cast as the villain 'frantically disguised in a long black cloak, black wig, spectacles and false teeth, and always photographed from the back'. He made his first talkie in 1932 and then only appeared three times on the screen – without much pleasure or acclaim – before making his Hollywood debut in 1952 in Joseph L. Mankiewicz's celebrated *Julius Caesar* with Marlon Brando and James Mason. Gielgud's portrayal of Cassius was a success, helped, of course, by the fact that he had already played the part on the stage. Inevitably he had to cut down on everything he'd done on the stage: 'I couldn't make the faces or give the shouts, and it was quite a different feeling. But I was much more in control of the part because I knew the whole line of it, each scene, even if there were cuts or scenes shot out of sequence.'

He returned to Shakespeare on the screen as Clarence in Olivier's *Richard III* in 1955, as Henry IV in Orson Welles' Falstaff hotchpotch *Chimes at Midnight* in 1966, and as Caesar himself in Stuart Burge's pedestrian version in 1969. For many years he found film work very unsatisfying: he never liked the early starts, and always found it difficult to give a cohesive shape and flow to his performance given the way pictures are shot piecemeal and rarely in chronological sequence. When *Chimes at Midnight* was first shown a friend told him that one of his most effective moments in the film came shortly after Hotspur's death when Gielgud looked first at Falstaff, next to Hotspur's body and then at Prince Hal – 'but we never did the scene at all. On the last day Orson said, "There's a close-up I have to do of you, just look down there, that's Hotspur's body, now look up at me." I never even saw Orson made up as Falstaff, but it appears that, because of the clever cutting, this scene of glances between four people is enormously effective. That shows how much you owe to the cutter and the director when it comes to the screen, you can't really control your own performance at all.'

In 1954 he was one of the forty-four guest stars Mike Todd persuaded to make cameo appearances in *Around the World in Eighty Days*. In 1956 the need to clear some surtax got the better of his judgement and he appeared as an overpowering and perverse Moulton Barrett in a dire remake of *The Barretts of Wimpole Street*. In the same year he played the Warwick in Otto Preminger's laborious version of *Saint Joan* with the ill-starred Jean Seberg. In 1963 he was cast as the French king Louis VII in the glossy Richard Burton/Peter O'Toole *Becket*, and earned himself an Oscar nomination. In 1964 he was one of the redeeming features of Tony Richardson's disappointing film of the Evelyn Waugh satire on the American way of death, *The Loved One*. By

Gielgud's first talking picture, Insult, *1932.*

the time he worked for Richardson again in 1967 in *The Charge of the Light Brigade* his film career was beginning to gather momentum.

The many pictures in which he has appeared since the late sixties have been of vastly varying quality. He must be the only theatrical knight to have appeared in pornography, the notorious Bob Guccione enterprise *Caligula*: 'They offered me the part of the Emperor Tiberius, and I turned it down, saying, "This is pure pornography." Gore Vidal, who wrote the original script, then wrote me a terrifically rude letter, saying how impertinent it was of me to refuse it and that if I knew what Tennessee Williams and Edward Albee said about me, I wouldn't be so grand. Terrible vituperation. Then they offered me another smaller part that wasn't dirty, and I rather shamefacedly took it. I played a whole scene in a bath of tepid water. It took three days to shoot and every two hours some terrible hags dragged me out, rubbed me down and put me back into the water again. Most extraordinary proceedings.'

With Jessie Matthews in The Good Companions, *1932.*

With Peter Lorre and Madeleine Carroll in The Secret Agent, *directed by Alfred Hitchcock, 1936.*

Below left: Gielgud as Disraeli with Fay Compton as Queen Victoria in The Prime Minister, *directed by Thorold Dickinson, 1940; and below: Gielgud as another Prime Minister, Lord Salisbury, in a Sherlock Holmes adventure,* Murder by Decree, *directed by Bob Clark, 1979.*

Filming Julius Caesar, *in 1952 with Marlon Brando and James Mason, (right) and (below) in 1969. The earlier productions, with Gielgud as Cassius directed by Joseph L. Mankiewicz, was a critical success. The second, with Gielgud as Caesar and directed by Stuart Burge, was not. 'It's terribly boring, film acting.'*

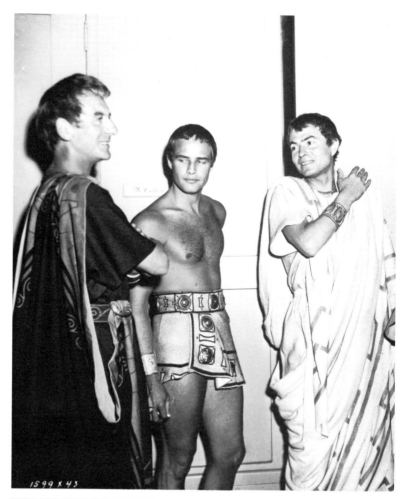

Left and below: Laurence Olivier with Gielgud on the set of Olivier's film version of Richard III, *1956; Gielgud played the Duke of Clarence.*

Noël Coward and John Gielgud, two of 'the cameo all-stars' in Mike Todd's film of Around the World in Eighty Days, *1956.*

Opposite: with Jennifer Jones and Virginia McKenna in The Barretts of Wimpole Street, *1956.*

With Jean Seberg in Otto Preminger's film version of Shaw's Saint Joan, *1957.*

With Richard Burton in Becket, *1964. Both Burton and Gielgud were nominated for Oscars for their performances, but neither was successful.*

Opposite: with Ralph Richardson in Oh! What a Lovely War, *1969; bottom left: with Jill Bennett in* The Charge of the Light Brigade, *1968; bottom right: as the Head of British Intelligence in* Mister Sebastian, *1967.*

Above: as Sharif El Gariani in Lion of the Desert, *1979; right: Gielgud the Pontiff in* The Shoes of the Fisherman, *1968.*

Above: in Tony Richardson's version of Evelyn Waugh's The Loved One, *1965.*

Left: Denis Quilley steals some rest while Gielgud steals yet another scene in the all-star Agatha Christie mystery Murder on the Orient Express, *1974.*

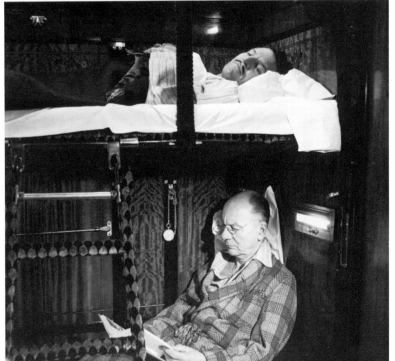

Opposite: with Malcolm McDowell on the set of Bob Guccione's Caligula, *1977. This was Gielgud's first (and last!) excursion into 'soft porn' and he, and most of the rest of the cast, had no idea what they were letting themselves in for.*

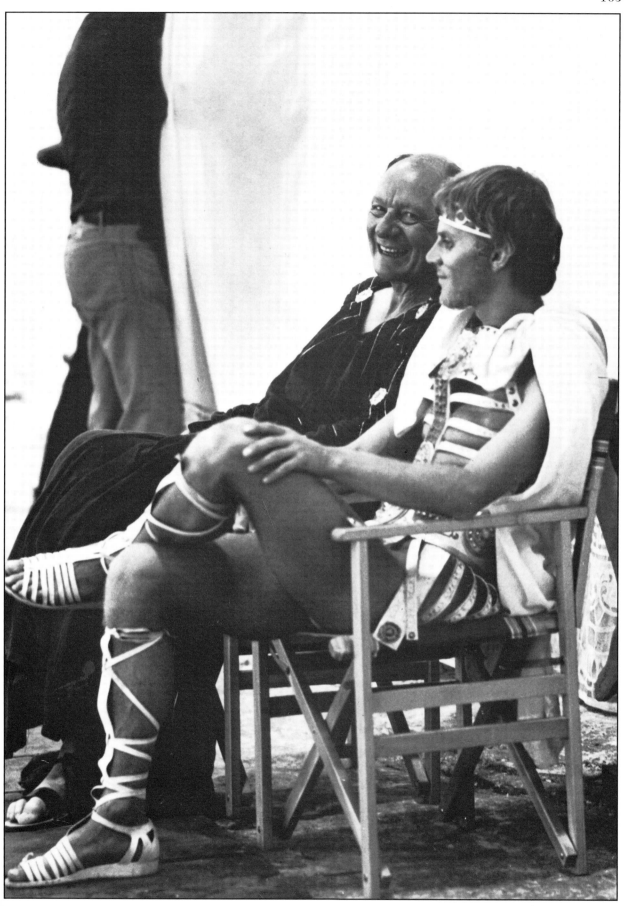

*Opposite: For his performance with
Dudley Moore and Liza Minelli in*
Arthur, *Gielgud earned his first
Hollywood Oscar.*

With Lindsay Anderson in Chariots of
Fire, *1981.*

Richardson, Olivier and Gielgud sharing a scene together for the first time – at the combined age of 233 – in Tony Palmer's film of Wagner, *1983.*

With Anthony Hopkins and Wendy Hiller in The Elephant Man, *1980.*

In several of the best of his more recent films – *The Elephant Man*, *Murder on the Orient Express*, *Chariots of Fire* – Gielgud gives beautifully telling cameo performances, but in only one or two has he had roles of sufficient size and scope to reveal him as a screen actor of the first magnitude. In 1976, working with David Mercer's script in Alain Resnais' film *Providence*, his performance was a revelation. 'Gielgud is superb' Peter Hall wrote at the time. 'Not only is his acting subtle and rich but his feelings are so great, his passion is so enormous, that he suggests heterosexuality in a way I would never have believed possible for him.'

And Stanley Kauffman, the Dean Swift of American film criticism, writing in *The New Republic*, was overwhelmed by his extraordinary vocal technique: 'What shading, what music – and never for its own sake. Everything he says is placed as if by divine order, the phrasing and pitch illuminating what he and the words are about. His lines here are studded with profanities, and in the mouth of this devilishly gleeful, highly articulate character, every one of them made me laugh. And to see him, ruddy-cheeked, bald-pated, big-nosed, treating each moment of life left to him like one more gob of pâté or gulp of wine, commenting on his pain like a spectator at a predictable black comedy – what a pleasure. What a *pleasure*.'

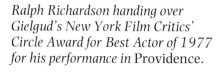

Ralph Richardson handing over Gielgud's New York Film Critics' Circle Award for Best Actor of 1977 for his performance in Providence.

Two Gielguds on stage together. Sir John reads Shakespeare and his niece, Maina Gielgud, dances, at a charity gala at the London Palladium, 1980.

Kauffman first saw Gielgud on the screen in *The Good Companions* in 1933 and, having watched him over the years in films and on stage, relished the development he felt privileged to have been able to witness. To look back on Gielgud's career gave him considerable pleasure: 'Part of the pleasure I get in that retrospect is in what he has done with himself technically: how what I first heard as a vibrant, somewhat too pressing voice has become a confident, easy instrument, greatly expanded in compass and greatly enriched in the quality of each note within that compass; how his movement, which had once included an often-parodied, heavy, almost pigeon-toed walk, was now smoothed and burnished at least to fit his needs without distraction. Part of my pleasure is in the fact that he is older and, as all interesting human beings do, has grown larger through living. And much of the

Above: With James Mason in The Shooting Party, *1984. Writing of James Mason, whose last film appearance this was, Iain Johnstone in the* Sunday Times *pronounced a verdict few would dispute: 'His encounter with Sir John Gielgud, who plays a dotty animal rights campaigner, is a brief but precious moment in the history of British Film.'; left: as Sir Leonard Darwin in* Plenty, *to be released in 1986.*

pleasure is in the patent evidence that, unlike so many gifted people, particularly gifted Americans, he has grown by living like an artist. I know nothing of his private life other than public rumour, and I don't care; I know something of the poor choices he has made in his career. Still he has become proof, irrefutable, that he thought of his life in relation to artistic purpose – with art as his centripetal force, his map, his reason for getting through each day and wanting to get up again next morning. Only an artist who gets serious joy out of shaping his life to nourish his art can finish like Gielgud.'

In 1982, exactly fifty years after making his first talking picture, John Gielgud was awarded his first Oscar. He won the Academy Award for Best Supporting Actor for the role of Hobson, the surrogate father, confidant and valet to playboy millionaire Dudley Moore in *Arthur*. It was a witty, knowing, wicked performance in an otherwise fairly flawed film, but whether or not it was really his greatest screen performance is irrelevant: in Hollywood terms it was his finest hour.

Through his many films, through his numerous television appearances, in the United States, even through his commercials for champagne, Gielgud has won himself a vast new audience, an audience, of course, that as likely as not has never seen him in his true setting: the theatre. Movie star, champagne salesman, eccentric darling of the chat shows, he may be seen to be as he embarks on his ninth incredible decade, but posterity will view him as he views himself: as a man of the theatre.

He once admitted that he had never understood politics or world affairs. 'I am lacking in ambition for power, large sums of money, or a passionate desire to convince other people that they are wrong and I am right,' he said in the early sixties, 'But I have a violent and sincere wish to be a good craftsman, and to understand what I try to do in the theatre, so as to be able to convince the people I work with.'

We may not see him on stage again in a major role – he shied away from a last assault on *Lear* at the National – but that is where his life has been spent and that is where his greatest achievements lie. The theatre is what he has known and loved all his life; it is, without exaggeration, what he has lived for. A few years ago when asked to talk about his proudest achievement, he replied: 'One thing I'm proud about in my career is the influence I've had on other actors who worked in my company, before the war particularly, and the general influence I've had in the theatre, because I am a very timid, shy, cowardly man out of it. But once I go into a theatre, I have great authority and I get great respect and love from all the people working in it – from the stagehands, the costumers, the scene designers and the actors – and this suddenly justifies your entire existence. I think that it is something that is much more precious to me than any personal success that I have had as an actor.'

Left: Yorkshire Television's production of Frankenstein, *in which Sir John played the blind hermit; overleaf, on the stage of the Old Vic at the party given by Gyles Brandreth and Pavilion Books to mark Sir John's eightieth birthday on 14 April, 1984.*

Stage Chronology · John Gielgud · Actor and Director

Theatre/Year	Play	Author	Role	Director
1921				
Old Vic	Henry V	Shakespeare	Herald	Robert Atkins
1922				
Old Vic	Peer Gynt	Ibsen	Walk on	Robert Atkins
Old Vic	King Lear	Shakespeare	Walk on	Robert Atkins
Old Vic	Wat Tyler	Halcott Glover	Walk on	Robert Atkins
On tour	The Wheel	J. B. Fagan	Lieut. Manners	J. B. Fagan
1923				
Regent	The Insect Play	Josef and Karel Capek	Felix, the Poet Butterfly	Nigel Playfair
Regent	Robert E. Lee	John Drinkwater	Aide de Camp	Nigel Playfair and John Drinkwater
Comedy	Charley's Aunt	Brandon Thomas	Charley	Amy Brandon-Thomas
1924				
Oxford Playhouse	Captain Brassbound's Conversion	Bernard Shaw	Johnson	Reginald Denham
Oxford Playhouse	Love For Love	William Congreve	Valentine	Reginald Denham
Oxford Playhouse	Mr Pim Passes By	A. A. Milne	Brian Strange	J. B. Fagan
Oxford Playhouse	She Stoops to Conquer	Oliver Goldsmith	Young Marlow	Reginald Denham
Oxford Playhouse	Monna Vanna	Maurice Maeterlinck	Prinzevalle	Reginald Denham
RADA	Romeo and Juliet	Shakespeare	Paris	
Regent	Romeo and Juliet	Shakespeare	Romeo	H.K. Ayliff
RADA	The Return Half	John van Druten	John Sherry	J. B. Fagan
Oxford Playhouse	Candida	Bernard Shaw	Marchbanks	J. B. Fagan
Oxford Playhouse	Deirdre of the Sorrows	J. M. Synge	Naisi	J. B. Fagan
Oxford Playhouse	A Collection Will Be Made	Arthur Eckersley	Paul Roget	J. B. Fagan
Oxford Playhouse	Everybody's Husband	Gilbert Cannan	A Domino	J. B. Fagan
Oxford Playhouse	The Cradle Song	Gregorio Martinez Sierra	Antonio	J. B. Fagan
Oxford Playhouse	John Gabriel Borkman	Ibsen	Erhart	J. B. Fagan
Oxford Playhouse	His Widow's Husband	Jacinto Benavente	Florencio	J. B. Fagan
Oxford Playhouse	Madame Pepita	Gregorio Martinez Sierra	Augusto	J. B. Fagan
1925				
Oxford Playhouse	A Collection Will Be Made	Arthur Eckersley	Paul Roget	J. B. Fagan
Oxford Playhouse	Smith	Somerset Maugham	Algernon	J. B. Fagan
Oxford Playhouse	The Cherry Orchard	Chekhov	Trofimov	J. B. Fagan
RADA	The Nature of the Evidence	Harold Peacey	Ted Hewitt	Guy Pelham Boulton
Aldwych (Phoenix Society)	The Orphan	Thomas Otway	Castalio	Allan Wade
Lyric, Hammersmith	The Cherry Orchard	Chekhov	Trofimov	J. B. Fagan
Royalty	The Cherry Orchard	Chekhov	Trofimov	J. B. Fagan
Little	The Vortex	Noël Coward	Nicky Lancaster	Noël Coward
Oxford Playhouse	The Lady from the Sea	Ibsen	A Stranger	J. B. Fagan
Oxford Playhouse	The Man with the Flower in His Mouth	Luigi Pirandello	Title part	J. B. Fagan
Little	The Seagull	Chekhov	Konstantin	A. E. Filmer
New Oxford (Phoenix Society)	Dr Faustus	Christopher Marlowe	Good Angel	Allan Wade
Little	Gloriana	Gwen John	Sir John Harrington	George Owen
Prince's (Play Actors)	L'Ecole des Cocottes	Paul Armant and Marcel Gerbidon	Robert	H. M. Harwood

Theatre/Year	Play	Author	Role	Director
1926 Savoy (matinees)	The Tempest	Shakespeare	Ferdinand	Henry Baynton
RADA	Sons and Fathers	Allan Monkhouse	Richard Southern	Milton Rosmer
Barnes	Three Sisters	Chekhov	Tuzenbach	Theodore Komisarjevsky
Barnes	Katerina	L. N. Andreyev	Georg	Theodore Komisarjevsky
Garrick	The Lady of the Camellias	A. Dumas *fils*	Armand	Sydney Bland
Court (300 Club)	Confession	W. F. Casey	Wilfred Marlay	Reginald Denham
New	The Constant Nymph	Margaret Kennedy and Basil Dean	Lewis Dodd	Basil Dean
1927 Apollo (Lyceum Club Stage Society)	Othello	Shakespeare	Cassio	A. E. Filmer
Strand (Stage Society)	The Great God Brown	Eugene O'Neill	Dion Anthony	Peter Godfrey
1928 Majestic, New York	The Patriot	Alfred Neumann	The Tsarevich	Gilbert Miller
Wyndham's (matinees)	Ghosts	Ibsen	Oswald	Peter Godfrey
Arts	Ghosts	Ibsen	Oswald	Peter Godfrey
Arts (matinee)	Prejudice	Mercedes de Acosta	Jacob Slovak	Leslie Banks
Globe	Holding Out the Apple	B. Wynne-Bower	Dr Gerald Marlowe	Leon M. Lion
Shaftesbury	The Skull	B. J. McOwen and H. E. Humphrey	Captain Allenby	Victor Morley
Court	The Lady From Alfaqueque	Serafin and Joaquin Alvarez Quintero	Felipe Rivas	James Whale
Court	Fortunato	Serafin and Joaquin Alvarez Quintero	Alberto	James Whale
Strand	Out of the Sea	Don Marquis	John Martin	Campbell Gullan and Henry Oscar
1929 Arts	The Seagull	Chekhov	Konstantin	A. E. Filmer
Little	Red Dust	V. M. Kirchow and A. V. Ouspensky	Fedor	Frank Vernon
Prince of Wales (Sunday Play Society)	Hunters Moon	Sophus Michaelis	Paul de Tressailles	Leslie Faber
Garrick	The Lady with a Lamp	Reginald Berkeley	Henry Tremayne	Leslie Banks and Edith Evans
Arts	Red Sunday	Hubert Griffith	Bronstein (Trotsky)	Theodore Komisarjevsky
Old Vic	Romeo and Juliet	Shakespeare	Romeo	Harcourt Williams
Old Vic	The Merchant of Venice	Shakespeare	Antonio	Harcourt Williams
Old Vic	The Imaginary Invalid	Molière	Cléante	Harcourt Williams
Old Vic	Richard II	Shakespeare	Richard II	Harcourt Williams
Old Vic	A Midsummer Night's Dream	Shakespeare	Oberon	Harcourt Williams
1930 Old Vic	Julius Caesar	Shakespeare	Mark Anthony	Harcourt Williams
Old Vic	As You Like It	Shakespeare	Orlando	Harcourt Williams
Old Vic	Androcles and the Lion	Bernard Shaw	The Emperor	Harcourt Williams with Edward Carrick
Old Vic	Macbeth	Shakespeare	Macbeth	Harcourt Williams
Old Vic	The Man with the Flower in his Mouth	Luigi Pirandello	Title part	Harcourt Williams
Old Vic	Hamlet	Shakespeare	Hamlet	Harcourt Williams
Queen's	Hamlet	Shakespeare	Hamlet	Harcourt Williams

Theatre/Year	Play	Author	Role	Director
Lyric, Hammersith	The Importance of Being Earnest	Oscar Wilde	John Worthing	Nigel Playfair
Old Vic	Henry IV, Part I	Shakespeare	Hotspur	Harcourt Williams
Old Vic	The Tempest	Shakespeare	Prospero	Harcourt Williams
Old Vic	The Jealous Wife	George Colman	Lord Trinket	Harcourt Williams
Old Vic	Antony and Cleopatra	Shakespeare	Antony	Harcourt Williams
1931 Sadler's Wells	Twelfth Night	Shakespeare	Malvolio	Harcourt Williams
Old Vic	Arms and the Man	Bernard Shaw	Sergius	Harcourt Williams
Old Vic	Much Ado About Nothing	Shakespeare	Benedick	Harcourt Williams
Old Vic	King Lear	Shakespeare	Lear	Harcourt Williams
His Majesty's	The Good Companions	J. B. Priestley and Edward Knoblock	Inigo Jollifant	Julian Wylie
1932 New, Oxford (OUDS)	Romeo and Juliet	Shakespeare	Director	
Criterion	Musical Chairs	Ronald Mackenzie	Joseph Schindler	Theodore Komisarjevsky
St Martin's	Strange Orchestra	Rodney Ackland	Director	
Old Vic	The Merchant of Venice	Shakespeare	Director	
1933 New	Richard of Bordeaux	Gordon Daviot	Richard, and co-Director	
Wyndham's	Sheppey	Somerset Maugham	Director	
1934 Shaftesbury	Spring 1600	Emlyn Williams	Director, and co-Producer	
New	Queen of Scots	Gordon Daviot	Director	
Wyndham's	The Maitlands	Ronald Mackenzie	Roger Maitland	Theodore Komisarjevsky
New	Hamlet	Shakespeare	Hamlet, and Director	
1935 New	The Old Ladies	Rodney Ackland	Director	
New	Noah	André Obey	Noah	Michel Saint-Denis
New	Romeo and Juliet	Shakespeare	Mercutio, and Director	
New	Romeo and Juliet	Shakespeare	Romeo, and Director	
1936 OUDS	Richard II	Shakespeare	Director	
New	The Seagull	Chekhov	Trigorin	Theodore Komisarjevsky
Alexandra, Toronto	Hamlet	Shakespeare	Hamlet	Guthrie McClintic
St James's, New York	Hamlet	Shakespeare	Hamlet	Guthrie McClintic
1937 Queen's	He Was Born Gay	Emlyn Williams	Mason, co-Director, and co-Producer	
Queen's	Richard II	Shakespeare	Richard, Director and Producer	
Queen's	The School for Scandal	Sheridan	Joseph Surface, and Producer	Tyrone Guthrie
1938 Queen's	Three Sisters	Chekhov	Vershinin, and Producer	Michel Saint-Denis
Queen's	The Merchant of Venice	Shakespeare	Shylock, co-Director and Producer	
Ambassadors'	Spring Meeting	M. J. Farrell and John Perry	Director	

Theatre/Year	Play	Author	Role	Director
Queen's	Dear Octopus	Dodie Smith	Nicholas	Glen Byam Shaw
1939 Globe	The Importance of Being Earnest	Oscar Wilde	John Worthing and Director	
Globe	Rhondda Roundabout	Jack Jones	Director	
Lyceum	Hamlet	Shakespeare	Hamlet, and Director	
Elsinore Castle	Hamlet	Shakespeare	Hamlet, and Director	
Globe	The Importance of Being Earnest	Oscar Wilde	John Worthing, and Director	
1940 Haymarket	The Beggar's Opera	John Gay	Director	
Old Vic	King Lear	Shakespeare	Lear	Lewis Casson and Harley Granville Barker
Old Vic	The Tempest	Shakespeare	Prospero	George Devine and Marius Goring
Globe on tour ENSA	Fumed Oak	Noël Coward	Henry Crow, and director	
Globe on tour ENSA	Hands Across the Sea	Noël Coward	Peter Gilpin, and director	
Globe on tour ENSA	Hard Luck Story	Chekhov	Old Actor, and director	
1941 Globe	Dear Brutus	J. M. Barrie	Will Dearth, and Director	
Apollo	Ducks and Drakes	M. J. Farrell	Director	
1942 Tour	Macbeth	Shakespeare	Macbeth, and Director	
Piccadilly	Macbeth	Shakespeare	Macbeth, and Director	
Phoenix	The Importance of Being Earnest	Oscar Wilde	John Worthing, and Director	
1943 Haymarket	The Doctor's Dilemma	Bernard Shaw	Louis Dubedat	Irene Hentschel
Phoenix and Haymarket	Love for Love	Congreve	Valentine, and Director	
Westminster	Landslide	Dorothy Albertyn and David Peel	Director	
1944 Apollo	The Cradle Song	Gregorio Martinez Sierra	Director	
Lyric	Crisis in Heaven	Eric Linklater	Director	
Phoenix	The Last of Summer	Kate O'Brien and John Perry	Director	
Tour	Hamlet	Shakespeare	Hamlet	George Rylands
Tour	Love for Love	Congreve	Valentine, Director	
Tour	The Circle	Somerset Maugham	Arnold Champion-Cheney	William Armstrong
Haymarket	The above three plays in repertoire			
1945 Haymarket	A Midsummer Night's Dream	Shakespeare	Oberon	Nevill Coghill
Haymarket	The Duchess of Malfi	John Webster	Ferdinand	George Rylands
Haymarket	Lady Windermere's Fan	Oscar Wilde	Director	
Far East Tour, ENSA	Hamlet	Shakespeare	Hamlet, and Director	

Theatre/Year	Play	Author	Role	Director
Far East Tour, ENSA	Blithe Spirit	Noël Coward	Charles Condomine and Director	
1946 New and Globe	Crime and Punishment	Rodney Ackland	Raskolnikoff	Anthony Quayle
1947 Royale, New York	The Importance of Being Earnest	Oscar Wilde	John Worthing, and Director	
US tour	Love for Love	Congreve	Valentine, and Director	
National, New York	Medea	Euripides	Jason, and Director	
National, New York	Crime and Punishment	Rodney Ackland	Raskolnikoff	Anthony Quayle
1948 Haymarket	The Glass Menagerie	Tennessee Williams	Director	
Globe	Medea	Euripides	Director	
Globe	The Return of the Prodigal	St John Hankin	Eustace Jackson	Peter Glenville
1949 Haymarket	The Heiress	Ruth and Augustus Goetz	Director	
Memorial, Stratford	Much Ado About Nothing	Shakespeare	Director	
Globe	The Lady's Not For Burning	Christopher Fry	Thomas Mendip, and Director	
Apollo	Treasure Hunt	M. J. Farrell and John Perry	Director	
1950 Lyric, Hammersmith	The Boy with a Cart	Christopher Fry	Director	
Lyric, Hammersith	Shall We Join the Ladies?	J. M. Barrie	Director	
Memorial, Stratford	Measure for Measure	Shakespeare	Angelo	Peter Brook
Memorial, Stratford	Julius Caesar	Shakespeare	Cassius	Anthony Quayle and Michael Langham
Memorial, Stratford	Much Ado About Nothing	Shakespeare	Benedick, and Director	
Memorial, Stratford	King Lear	Shakespeare	Lear, and co-Director	
1951 Royale, New York	The Lady's Not For Burning	Christopher Fry	Thomas Mendip, and Director	
Phoenix	The Winter's Tale	Shakespeare	Leontes	Peter Brook
1952 Phoenix	Much Ado About Nothing	Shakespeare	Benedick, and Director	
Memorial, Stratford	Macbeth	Shakespeare	Director	
Lyric, Hammersith	Richard II	Shakespeare	Director	
1953 Lyric, Hammersith	The Way of the World	Congreve	Mirabell, and Director	
Lyric, Hammersith	Venice Preserv'd	Thomas Otway	Jaffier	Peter Brook
Bulawayo	Richard II	Shakespeare	Richard, and Director	
Haymarket	A Day by the Sea	N. C. Hunter	Julian Anson, and Director	
1954 New	Charley's Aunt	Brandon Thomas	Director	
Lyric, Hammersmith	The Cherry Orchard	Chekhov, adapted John Gielgud	Director	
1955 Memorial, Stratford	Twelfth Night	Shakespeare	Director	
European Tour	King Lear	Shakespeare	Lear, and co-Director	

Theatre/Year	Play	Author	Role	Director
Palace	Much Ado About Nothing	Shakespeare	Benedick, and Director	
Palace	King Lear	Shakespeare	Lear, and co-Director	
European tour	The two plays above			
1956 Haymarket	The Chalk Garden	Enid Bagnold	Director	
Globe	Nude with Violin	Noël Coward	Sebastian, and Director	
1957 Covent Garden	The Trojans	Berlioz	Director	
Memorial, Stratford	The Tempest	Shakespeare	Prospero	Peter Brook
Tour	The Ages of Man	Shakespeare	Anthology	
Drury Lane	The Tempest	Shakespeare	Prospero	Peter Brook
1958 Globe	The Potting Shed	Graham Greene	James Callifer	Michael MacOwan
Globe	Variation on a Theme	Terence Rattigan	Director	
Old Vic	Henry VIII	Shakespeare	Wolsey	Michael Benthall
Tour of USA, Canada	The Ages of Man	Shakespeare	Anthology	
46th Street, New York	The Ages of Man	Shakespeare	Anthology	
1959 Globe	The Complaisant Lover	Graham Greene	Director	
Queen's	The Ages of Man	Shakespeare	Anthology	
US tour	Much Ado About Nothing	Shakespeare	Director	
Music Box, New York	Five Finger Exercise	Peter Shaffer	Director	
1960 Phoenix	The Last Joke	Enid Bagnold	Prince Ferdinand	Glen Byam Shaw
1961 Covent Garden	A Midsummer Night's Dream	Michael Tippett	Director	
ANTA, New York	Big Fish, Little Fish	Hugh Wheeler	Director	
Globe	Dazzling Prospect	M. J. Farrell and John Perry	Director	
Royal Shakespeare, Stratford	Othello	Shakespeare	Othello	Franco Zeffirelli
Aldwych	The Cherry Orchard	Chekhov	Gaev	Michel Saint-Denis
1962 Haymarket	The School for Scandal	Sheridan	Director	
Haymarket	The School for Scandal	Sheridan	Joseph Surface, and Director	
Majestic, New York	The School for Scandal	Sheridan	Joseph Surface, and Director	
1963 Majestic, New York	Seven Ages of Man			
Haymarket	The Ides of March	Thornton Wilder	Caesar, and co-Director	
1964 Lunt-Fontanne, New York	Hamlet	Shakespeare	Ghost (recorded), and Director	
World tour	The Ages of Man			
Billy Rose, New York	Tiny Alice	Edward Albee	Julian	Alan Schneider
1965 Phoenix	Ivanov	Chekhov, adapted John Gielgud	Ivanov, and Director	
1966 US tour	Ivanov	Chekhov, adapted John Gielgud	Ivanov, and Director	

Theatre/Year	Play	Author	Role	Director
Shubert, New York	Ivanov	Chekhov, adapted John Gielgud	Ivanov, and Director	
1967				
US tour	The Ages of Man			
Queen's	Halfway Up the Tree	Peter Ustinov	Director	
Old Vic (NT)	Tartuffe	Molière	Orgon	Tyrone Guthrie
1968				
Old Vic (NT)	Oedipus	Seneca, adapted Ted Hughes	Oedipus	Peter Brook
Coliseum	Don Giovanni	Mozart	Director	
Apollo	Forty Years On	Alan Bennett	Headmaster	Patrick Garland
1970				
Lyric	The Battle of Shrivings	Peter Shaffer	Sir Gideon Petrie	Peter Hall
Royal Court	Home	David Storey	Harry	Lindsay Anderson
Morosco, New York	Home	David Storey	Harry	Lindsay Anderson
1971				
Chichester	Caesar and Cleopatra	Bernard Shaw	Caesar	Robin Phillips
1972				
Royal Court	Veterans	Charles Wood	Sir Geoffrey Kendle	Ronald Eyre
Queen's	Private Lives	Noël Coward	Director	
1973				
Albery	The Constant Wife	Somerset Maugham	Director	
1974				
Old Vic (NT)	The Tempest	Shakespeare	Prospero	Peter Hall
Royal Court	Bingo	Edward Bond	Shakespeare	Jane Howell and John Dove
1975				
Old Vic (NT)	No Man's Land	Harold Pinter	Spooner	Peter Hall
Albery	The Gay Lord Quex	Arthur Pinero	Director	
Wyndhams (NT)	No Man's Land	Harold Pinter	Spooner	Peter Hall
1976				
Old Vic (NT)	Tribute to the Lady	devised Val May		Val May
Lyttelton	No Man's Land	Harold Pinter	Spooner	Peter Hall
Longacre, New York	No Man's Land	Harold Pinter	Spooner	Peter Hall
1977				
Lyttelton	No Man's Land	Harold Pinter	Spooner	Peter Hall
Olivier	Julius Caesar	Shakespeare	Caesar	John Schlesinger
Olivier	Volpone	Ben Jonson	Sir Politic Would-Be	Peter Hall
Cottesloe	Half-Life	Julian Mitchell	Sir Noel Cunliffe	Waris Hussein
1978				
Duke of York's	Half-Life	Julian Mitchell	Sir Noel Cunliffe	Waris Hussein

Film and Television Chronology · Major Roles

Date	Film (TV)	Role	Director
1924	Who is the Man?	Daniel	Walter Summers
1929	The Clue of the New Pin	Rex Trasmere	Arthur Maude
1932	Insult	Henri Dubois	Harry Lachman
1933	The Good Companions	Inigo Jollifant	Victor Saville
1936	The Secret Agent	Edgar Brodie	Alfred Hitchcock
1941	The Prime Minister	Benjamin Disraeli	Thorold Dickinson
1953	Julius Caesar	Cassius	Joseph Mankiewicz
1955	Richard III	Clarence	Laurence Olivier

Date	Film (TV)	Role	Director
1957	Around the World in 80 Days	Foster	Michael Anderson
	The Barretts of Wimpole Street	Edward Moulton Barrett	Sidney Franklin
	Saint Joan	Warwick	Otto Preminger
1959	A Day by the Sea (TV)	Julian Anson	
	The Browning Version (TV)	Andrew Crocker Harris	
1963	The Rehearsal (TV)	The Count	
1964	Becket	Louis VII	Peter Glenville
1966	The Loved One	Sir Francis Hinsley	Tony Richardson
	Chimes at Midnight	Henry IV	Orson Welles
	Alice in Wonderland (TV)	Mock Turtle	Jonathan Miller
	The Mayfly and the Frog (TV)	Gabriel Kantara	
1967	From Chekhov with Love (TV)	Chekhov	
	Mister Sebastian	Head of British Intelligence	David Greene
	The Charge of the Light Brigade	Lord Raglan	Tony Richardson
1968	The Shoes of the Fisherman	The Elder Pope	Michael Anderson
	Saint Joan (TV)	The Inquisitor	
	Oh! What a Lovely War	Count Berchtold	Richard Attenborough
1969	In Good King Charles's Golden Days (TV)	King Charles	
	Conversation at Night (TV)	The Writer	Rudolf Cartier
1970	Julius Caesar	Caesar	Stuart Burge
	Eagle in a Cage	Lord Sissal	Fielder Cook
	Hassan (TV)	The Caliph	
	Hamlet (TV)	The Ghost	
1973	Lost Horizon	Chang	Charles Jarrott
1974	11 Harrowhouse	Meecham	Aram Avakian
	Gold	Farrell	Peter Hunt
	Murder on the Orient Express	Beddoes	Sidney Lumet
1976	The Picture of Dorian Gray	Lord Wotton	
	Aces High	Headmaster	Jack Gold
1977	Providence	Clive Langham	Alain Resnais
	Heartbreak House (TV)	Captain Shotover	
	A Portrait of the Artist as a Young Man	Preacher	Joseph Strick
1979	Murder by Decree	Lord Salisbury	Bob Clark
1980	The Elephant Man	Carr Gomm	David Lynch
	Caligula	Nerva	Tinto Brass
1981	The Lion of the Desert	Sharif El Gariani	Moustapha Akkad
	Arthur	Hobson	Steve Gordon
	Chariots of Fire	Master of Trinity	David Puttnam
1983	Wagner	Pfistermeister	Tony Palmer
	Gandhi	Lord Irwin	Richard Attenborough
	Scandalous	Hogarth	Rob Cohen
	The Wicked Lady	Hogarth	Michael Winner
	Brideshead Revisited (TV)	Edward Ryder	Charles Sturridge and Michael Lindsay-Hogg
1984	The Far Pavilions (TV)	Cavagnari	Peter Duffell
	The Shooting Party	Cornelius Cardew	Alan Bridges
	Frankenstein (TV)	De Lacey	
	Camille (TV)	The Duke	
	Plenty	Sir Leonard Darwin	Fred Schepisi
	Romance on the Orient Express (TV)	Charles Woodward	Lawrence Gordon Clark

Bibliography

The dates refer to the year of publication of the edition used by the author.

Agate, James: *Brief Chronicles* (1943)
   Red Letter Nights (1945)
   The Contemporary Theatre 1944–5 (1946)
Beaumont, Tim (ed.): *The Selective Ego* (1976)
Anthony, Gordon: *John Gielgud, Camera Studies by Gordon Anthony with an Introduction by Michel Saint-Denis* (1938)
Buckle, Richard (ed.): *The Selected Diaries of Cecil Beaton* (1979)
Bishop, George W.: *My Betters* (1957)
Burton, Hal (ed.): *Great Acting* (1967)
Casson, John: *Lewis and Sybil – A Memoir* (1972)
Curtis, Anthony: *The Rise and Fall of the Matinée Idol* (1974)
Farjeon, Herbert: *The Shakespearean Scene* (1949)
Findlater, Richard: *These Our Actors* (1983)
Funke, Lewis and Booth, John E.: *Actors Talk about Acting* (1961)
Gielgud, John: *An Actor and his Time* (1979)
   Distinguished Company (1972)
   Early Stages (1939)
   Stage Directions (1963)
Gilder, Rosamond: *John Gielgud's Hamlet* (1937)
Goodwin, John (ed.): Peter Hall's Diaries (1973)
Guthrie, Tyrone: *A Life in the Theatre* (1959)
Hall, Peter: *Peter Hall's Diaries*, edited by John Goodwin (1983)
Hayman, Ronald: *John Gielgud* (1971)
Kauffmann, Stanley: *Before my Eyes* (1974)
Mander, Raymond and Mitchenson, Joe: *Hamlet through the Ages* (1952)
Marowitz, C., Milne, T., and Hale, O.: *The Encore Reader* (1965)
Nichols, Beverley: *The Unforgiving Minute* (1978)
Nicolson, Harold: *Diaries and Letters* 1930–39 (1966)
Olivier, Laurence: *Confessions of an Actor* (1982)
Payn, Graham and Morley, Sheridan (ed.): *The Noël Coward Diaries* (1982)
Redfield, William, *Letters from an Actor* (1966)
Redgrave, Michael: *In My Mind's Eye* (1983)
Sinden, Donald: *A Touch of the Memoirs* (1982)
Speaight, Robert: *Shakespeare on Stage* (1973)
Stern, Richard L., *John Gielgud directs Richard Burton in Hamlet* (1967)
Trewin, J. C.: *A Play Tonight* (1952)
   The Theatre since 1900 (1951)
Trewin, J. C., Mander, Raymond and Mitchenson, Joe: *The Gay Twenties – A Decade of the Theatre* (1958)
Tynan, Kenneth: *Curtains* (1961)
   He that Plays the King (1950)
   The Sound of Two Hands Clapping (1975)
Ustinov, Peter: *Dear Me* (1977)
Williams, Emlyn: *Emlyn* (1973)
Williams, Harcourt: *Four Years at the Old Vic* (1935)
   Old Vic Saga (1949)
Williamson, Audrey: *Old Vic Drama* (1948)
Wolfit, Donald: *First Interval* (1954)

Acknowledgements

This book has been designed as a pictorial tribute to the life and work of Sir John Gielgud and as such it would have been impossible to compile without the invaluable help of the legendary Raymond Mander and Joe Mitchenson Theatre Collection. My debt to them, to the book's designer Craig Dodd, to my indefatigable editor Judy Dauncey and her associate picture researcher Mia Stewart-Wilson, is considerable. I would also like to thank Angus McBean, Edward Thompson, Mary Wilson of the Shakespeare Birthplace Trust, Sheila Formoy of H.M. Tennent Limited, Louis Frewer and Martin Jarvis for their kind assistance.

In telling the story of Sir John's career I have wherever possible used the words of eyewitnesses. I have quoted most of the leading critics of the day and many of Sir John's colleagues and friends, and I am grateful to the authors and publishers of the books listed in the bibliography for permission to reproduce extracts from them. The chronology of Sir John's stage work is based upon the one in Richard Findlater's admirable book, *These Our Actors* (Elm Tree, 1983). My quotations from Sir John are taken from his own published reminiscences and from a wide variety of interviews given by him between 1932 and 1983. I have relied particularly on those given by him to John Boothe and Lewis Funke, Cyril Butcher, Gerald Clarke, Derek Hart, Harold Hobson, Peter Roberts and George Rylands. Above all, of course, I am indebted to Sir John himself for allowing me to reproduce copyright material and personal photographs.

BBC: 147 (below), 149, 150; Condé Nast: (Norman Parkinson) 104; Donald Cooper: 137 (below), 141, 142, 143 (below), 145 (top); Zoë Dominic: 6, 111, 112, 113, 114, 117, 124, 133, 136, 137 (top), 168; Clive Francis: 1; Louis Frewer: 19; Friedman-Abeles: 130, 131; Granada Television: 144; Hirschfeld: 145 (below); David Hockney: 2; Imperial War Museum: 82 (lower left); Kobal Collection: 151, 152, 153, 154, 155 (top), 156 (right), 157, 160 (top and below right), 161, 162 (below), 163, 164 (above), 165, 166 (below); Raymond Mander and Joe Mitchenson Theatre Collection: 15, 16, 17, 18, 21, 22, 23, 24, 25, 27, 28, 29, 30, 33, 34, 35 (top), 36, 37, 39, 40, 41, 43, 44, 45, 47, 48, 49, 51, 53, 54 (Cecil Beaton), 60 (top), 65 (Angus McBean), 72, 74, 75, 76, 77 (below), 78, 79, 82 (right, top and below), 84, 85, 86, 87, 97 (Angus McBean), 101, 105, 107, 109, 115, 122, 123; Angus McBean: 91, 93, 94, (top), 95, 96, 98, 99, 100, 110, (right), 119, 120, 121; National Portrait Gallery: 59, (Howard Coster) 60 (below), (Howard Coster) 62; National Film Archive: 158, 159, 160 (below left), 162 (top), 164 (below), 166 (above); Punch magazine: 139 (left); Radio Times Hulton Picture Library: 31, 35 (below), 38, 42, 52, 68, 69, 70, 71, 81, 88, 94 (below), 102, 103, 106 (left), 110 (left), 126, 127, 128, 140, 146, 147 (top), 156 (left), 167; Geoffrey Reeve Productions: 169 (top); Rex Features: 155 (below); Royal Opera House: 125 (top); S & G Agency: 106 (right); Sothebys Belgravia (Cecil Beaton), 55, 58, 83, 89; Stoll Theatres: 134; Syndication International: 148; Tatler magazine: 66; Theatre Museum, Victoria & Albert Museum: 50, 56, 78, 82 (top left), Houston Rogers 125 (below), 135; Thorn EMI Screen Entertainment: 169 (below); John Timbers: 118, 138; John Vickers: 77, (top); Reg Wilson: 143 (top); Yorkshire Television Limited: 170.

The publisher has endeavoured to acknowledge all copyright holders of the pictures reproduced in this book. However, in view of the complexity of securing copyright information, should any photographs not be correctly attributed, then the publisher undertakes to make any appropriate changes in future editions of this book.

Index

Page numbers in italics refer to illustrations